For Brenda

MW00576038

Do Not Separate Her from Her Garden

Carolyn Ferrari 4·18·23

Do Not Separate 'HER' from HER GARDEN

ANNE SPENCER'S ECOPOETICS

CARLYN ENA FERRARI

UNIVERSITY OF VIRGINIA PRESS

Charlottesville and London

University of Virginia Press
© 2022 by the Rector and Visitors of the University of Virginia
All rights reserved
Printed in the United States of America on acid-free paper

First published 2022

1 3 5 7 9 8 6 4 2

Library of Congress Cataloging-in-Publication Data

Names: Ferrari, Carlyn Ena, author.
Title: Do not separate her from her garden : Anne Spencer's ecopoetics /
Carlyn Ena Ferrari.
Description: Charlottesville : University of Virginia Press, 2022. |
Includes bibliographical references and index.
Identifiers: LCCN 2022014508 (print) | LCCN 2022014509 (ebook) |
ISBN 9780813948768 (hardcover) | ISBN 9780813948775 (paperback) |
ISBN 9780813948782 (ebook)
Subjects: LCSH: Spencer, Anne, 1882–1975—Criticism and interpretation. |
Spencer, Anne, 1882–1975—Philosophy. | Spencer, Anne, 1882–1975—Homes
and haunts. | Nature in literature. | Ecology in literature. | Feminism in
literature. | American literature—African American authors—History and
criticism. | American literature—Women authors—History and criticism.
Classification: LCC PS3537.P444 Z64 2022 (print) | LCC PS3537.P444
(ebook) | DDC 811/.52—dc23/eng/20220616
LC record available at https://lccn.loc.gov/2022014508
LC ebook record available at https://lccn.loc.gov/2022014509

Cover art: Anne Spencer in her garden. (Papers of Anne Spencer and
the Spencer Family, 1829, 1864–2007, #14204, Special Collections,
University of Virginia Library, Charlottesville, Va.; courtesy of the
Anne Spencer House and Garden Museum, Inc., Archives)

For my mother, Ena Gracia Ferrari,
who taught me how to read when I was three,
and for her mother, Francine Delva Gracia,
who never learned how

Contents

Acknowledgments

I find it incredibly daunting to try to name all the individuals for whom I am grateful. It seems more appropriate to offer an apology because the page and my words are simply inadequate and insufficient to offer gratitude to everyone who has helped me complete this work and become the woman I am today. I am as grateful for anyone who has made me smile as I am to those who have read my work because both gestures acknowledge and affirm my personhood. With that caveat in mind, I want to begin by thanking my mother for supporting my personal and professional dreams. You are the most brilliant person I know. Even though you may not have understood or agreed with my aspirations, you dared me to dream even bigger, and you remind me that I am more than enough. Merci pour tout. Que Dieu vous benisse. I want to thank my brothers, Leo, Pierre Philip, and Mario, for their love and for letting me be their "favorite sister."

I extend a very special thank-you to Dr. Steven Tracy for introducing me to Anne Spencer as a graduate student. Thank you for making Spencer "half my world." I want to thank Drs. James Smethurst, Mecca Sullivan, and Kevin Quashie for continuing to mentor and support my intellectual and professional endeavors and demystifying academia. Much of this book was written during the COVID-19 pandemic, so I thank those who lifted me out moments of crippling panic, anxiety, and depression. To Kelly N. Giles, thank you for loving and accepting me *because* of who I am, not despite who I am. It is an honor to critically engage with you. To McKinley E. Melton, your friendship is a gift and a blessing; it has comforted and sustained me in ways that I did not know were possible.

These individuals have held space for me—personally, professionally, and intellectually—as I have written this book, and I am grateful to them for lifting me up and letting me be: Ernest Allen, J. T. Roane, Peter Blackmer, Keyona Jones, Donna Freitas, Jennifer Fleischner, Jacqueline Jones LaMon, Judith Baumel, Kelly Swartz, Jacqueline Olvera, and Rani Varghese. To my friends in California—Stephanie May, Heather Lambeth, Jasmin Montgomery, Maria

Rankin-Brown, Morris Brown, Clay Klein, and Janie Korbel—you encouraged me when I was homesick and reminded me that academia is what I do, not who I am. I am grateful to Andrew and Kerene Ogot for providing love and a sense of family and home while I lived on the East Coast. To Dr. Sarita Cannon, you expanded the contours of my imagination and helped me realize that it was possible to be a Black woman in the academy.

This book would not have been possible without generous research support, so I thank the Provost's Office and the College of Arts and Sciences Dean's Office at Seattle University. I also extend my gratitude to the W. E. B. Du Bois Center at the University of Massachusetts Amherst Libraries, the Institute for Citizens and Scholars Career Enhancement Fellowship, and the William A. Elwood Fellowship in Civil Rights and African-American Studies at the University of Virginia for the support and faith in my scholarship. I thank the archivists at the Albert and Shirley Small Special Collections Library at the University of Virginia for their expertise and careful preservation of Anne Spencer's papers. I am grateful for my current colleagues at Seattle University, who have shown much grace and offered community amid my challenging transition during the pandemic. I thank my students—past, present, and future—who make me want to be a better scholar, educator, and human.

I offer my humble gratitude to Shaun Spencer-Hester, Anne Spencer's granddaughter and executive director/curator at the Anne Spencer Memorial Foundation, Inc./The Anne Spencer House and Garden Museum, Inc., for the personal tour and incredible insight she offered when I visited the Spencer home and for her tireless efforts to keep Anne Spencer's legacy alive. I also thank Ms. Spencer-Hester for granting me the permissions to reprint Anne Spencer's poetry and unpublished writings here.

To the editor of this work, Eric Brandt, thank you for your patience and commitment; my gratitude also extends to the University of Virginia Press editorial team; to the anonymous readers of this work, I am grateful for their generous engagement, careful appraisal, and keen insight. Portions of the second chapter of this book appeared in the article "Anne Spencer's 'Natural' Poetics," *College Language Association Journal* 61, no. 4 (2018): 185–200. I thank the editors for letting me reprint my work here. This book's afterword originally appeared as an essay in *CONSEQUENCE Online,* October 21, 2020.

I will be eternally grateful to Janet Jackson and Prince for the poetics of *Rhythm Nation* and Paisley Park.

And, of course, I thank Anne Spencer for being. Amen.

Preface

I grew up seeing my father spend his afternoons and evenings in his garden. He would watch his plants, talk to his plants, or just sit in their stillness. The most-coveted household chore was watering his plants because of the responsibility that came with it. His garden was—and still is—his most prized possession.

I had the privilege of growing up in the San Francisco Bay Area and seeing a Black man deeply connected to the natural world. The natural world occupied a sacred space in our home because it was sacred to my father. We learned how to properly sort our household waste for home composting, and we welcomed new plants with joy and anticipation as one would welcome a new child.

My father was known for his garden. Friends and family members looked forward to the plum and apple harvests, especially. They were always so sweet. We were a family of six, so we outgrew our small home rather quickly, but we never moved.

But where will he garden? my mother would ask after touring a new home that seemed promising. I understand now what she was really asking: *But how will he express himself? How will he be?*

My father is a stoic man. Gardening is how he expresses his emotion and is an extension of who he is in this world.

Our relationship has always been complicated. We are generations and cultures apart. He, a traditional Caribbean man, has an outspoken Black feminist for a daughter. He wants me to listen; I want him to hear me.

As I write this, I realize that my father primed me for what would become my intellectual endeavor. As a scholar, I am interested in how Black writers theorize and make meaning of the natural world, so it makes sense that I was drawn to Anne Spencer. I often remark that I had never seen a connection to the natural world quite like hers. But that is not true. I have seen this type of intimacy my entire life.

My father's garden is half his world. And for that I am grateful because it enabled me to bear witness to Anne Spencer's way of being in the world.

Do Not Separate Her from Her Garden

Introduction

Anne Spencer's (Re)Vision of Nature

"I do not separate you from your garden, your elegant verse and your sure philosophy."[1] Georgia Douglas Johnson penned these words in a February 1951 letter to her close friend and fellow New Negro Renaissance writer Anne Spencer. Johnson's words are not only a testament to the centrality of Spencer's garden within her life, but also they serve as a plea and a commandment: one should not separate Spencer from her garden. The natural world was Spencer's muse, her mediator, her sanctuary, her legacy, and an extension of herself. My study heeds Johnson's imperative and bridges the discourse on Black female writers' self-representation and literary ecocriticism to illustrate how Spencer's poetics are infused with natural world imagery that enables her to both articulate her own ecological appreciation and map the experiences of Black womanhood onto the natural world. Spencer's writing and her garden shared a symbiotic relationship. However, her garden was more than just her muse; it was also her mantra.

Despite Anne Spencer's inclusion in several major literary anthologies and her efforts as a cultural organizer of the New Negro Renaissance, she has received minimal scholarly attention and critical engagement as either a New Negro Renaissance figure or a Black female poet. The few scholars who have engaged with Spencer's work have mostly consulted her poetry. This book helps to close the existing critical silence surrounding her body of work and introduce Spencer as a prose writer, showcasing her unknown and unpublished prose works. These previously overlooked materials position Spencer not just as a forgotten New Negro artist but also as an unsung twentieth-century Black intellectual and key forerunner to the Black Arts Movement and Black feminist writers. My research centers Spencer's published and unpublished prose to demonstrate both the range of Spencer's artistry and the degree to which her relationship with the natural world informed both her poetics and personal politics. In this work, I employ *ecopoetics* to discuss the way Spencer's writing is infused with her ideologies on Black womanhood and the environment. My critical engagement with Spencer's poetry facilitates new readings of the natural world within Black women's literature and highlights ecocriticism's failure to take race, gender, and sexuality fully into account.

Do Not Separate Her from Her Garden celebrates Anne Spencer's life; however, it is not a biography. The primary aim of this book is to analyze Spencer's body of work alongside her relationship with the natural world. The secondary aim of this volume is to demonstrate the apertures created through ecocritical readings of Black women's writings. Spencer belongs to a rich tradition of Black women writers who summoned natural world symbols as a vehicle through which to communicate their multiple oppressions. I position ecocritical readings as an overlooked site of inquiry through which we may enrich our understanding of Black women's discursive strategies and self-representation. For Spencer, the natural world is liberatory and a means to transcend circumscribed notions of Black womanhood, and it is also the lens through which she both views and theorizes the world around her. Spencer draws on nature as a symbol for what is beautiful, stable, and normative; however, she is not interested in reproducing and mobilizing the norm. By deploying an ecological consciousness, she expands the possibilities of Black womanhood and sexuality and offers alternative, expansive visions of Black womanhood. Spencer's garden is both a literal space and a powerful symbol of possibility. As a haven she creates for herself, her garden represents her audacity to engage in a form of space-making and negotiating to combat racial and gender oppression. As a poetic symbol, her garden becomes an invitation for Black women to create metaphorical gardens of their own. By inserting her garden into her poetry, she makes the claim that this type of self-fashioned, space-making pleasure should be enjoyed by all Black women. Simultaneously corrupted by white male oppression yet unfettered, the natural world served as a fitting symbol for Spencer to both articulate the depth of Black women's oppression and imagine their freedom. Spencer's writings illustrate that she is acutely aware of the importance of self-fashioned pleasure in her life as a Black woman. However, she is not only concerned with Black women's survival. She is also concerned with their happiness, which she claims is their right.

Central to this project is J. Lee Greene's 1977 biographical text *Time's Unfading Garden: Anne Spencer's Life and Poetry*, which serves as the only significant account of Spencer's life and artistry. It is also crucial to note that this biographical text also serves as the most comprehensive collections of Spencer's poetry.[2] Spencer penned thousands of poems and prose pieces, many of which are undated; however, only approximately thirty of her poems are published. Greene beautifully captures the complexity of Spencer's life, weaving together her civil rights activism, love of gardening, and prolific (unpublished) writing. Greene demonstrates that at the core of Spencer's poetry is an intimate appreciation for natural beauty: "The thrust of Anne Spencer's poetry is her belief in the world that beauty gives us inklings of—intimations which we must cultivate like a garden. Thus her poetry and her garden are manifestations of the same principle of creativity" (107–8). Greene underscores the significance of Spencer's garden to both her writing and existential well-being, and this book elaborates on his work by making explicit the relationship between Spencer's passion for gardening and the natural world and her formal poetic choices.

In spite of the New Negro Renaissance being a pivotal African American artistic and cultural movement, women's contributions were largely negated and overlooked prior to the late 1980s and 1990s until works by such Black feminist scholars as Deborah McDowell, Maureen Honey, Gloria (Akasha) Hull, and Cheryl A. Wall recontextualized New Negro Renaissance women writers and revealed their centrality.[3] Though Spencer's poetry has received minimal scholarly attention and critical engagement, she both wrote and published during the New Negro Movement, and her Lynchburg, Virginia, home was a heavily frequented literary salon. Her discursive strategies and representations of the Black female body parallel those of the more "canonical" New Negro women writers such as Nella Larsen and Jessie Fauset, who advocated for the New Negro woman's right to happiness, self-determinism, and pleasure and penned novels and short stories that focused on self-determined Black female protagonists. When situated within the context of the New Negro Renaissance, Spencer's writing is highly subversive in its undaunted Black feminist politics (and arguably even more overtly subversive than her critically acclaimed contemporaries). My research expands the work of historian Erin D. Chapman's text *Prove It on Me: New Negroes, Sex, and Popular Culture in the 1920s,* which illustrates how New Negro women writers, such as Jessie Redmon Fauset, Nella Larsen, and Marita Bonner, utilized the "domestic sphere" of writing to create fiction that allowed them to transcend the prescriptive sexual and social mores of New Negro womanhood and express their wholeness and sexual self-determination. Spencer's discursive strategies, however, often relied on her own personal views and personal life, not fictional representations. Thus, for Spencer, the personal was political, and I extend Chapman's important work on New Negro women's discursive strategies by arguing that Spencer's discursive strategies and representations of Black womanhood parallel those of her New Negro Renaissance female contemporaries.

The limited scholarship on Spencer does little to establish her as a Black feminist theorist in her own right and does not consider the centrality of her garden to her life or writing. This scholarship reduces Spencer to her seemingly simple political and formal inclinations, labeling her either a "feminist" or a "modernist." Scholars Erlene Stetson and Charita M. Ford identified a feminist poetics in Spencer's writing and accurately recognized her as an early Black feminist in the late 1970s and 1980s, respectively. Stetson's and Ford's scholarship has been largely unanswered, but in recent years and since the University of Virginia's acquisition of the Papers of Anne Spencer and the Spencer Family in 2008, slight interest has been generated. In her 2012 article "'Chatterton, Shelley, Keats and I': Reading Anne Spencer in the White Literary Tradition," poet Holly Karapetkova cautions against the hasty dismissal of Spencer's work and claims that her poetic choices were "profoundly modern, black, and female" (229). Similarly, in her 2015 article "Anne Spencer's Feminist Modernist Poetics," scholar Jenny Hyest extends this analysis and contends that a symbiotic relationship existed between her feminist politics and experimental style, suggesting that her feminist poetics "necessitated her modernism" (131). Such conclusions are accurate and indeed supported by Spencer's poetry; however, Spencer did not view her writing and her politics in such compartmentalized terms. For Spencer, writing was not just a hobby; it was an existential practice.

Spencer's prose writings, though largely unpublished, contain profound meditations on a wide array of subjects pertaining to gender relations, "the Negro problem," and the natural world, positioning her as both a cultural theorist and early environmentalist. Spencer's poetry often left critics confounded or unmoved and was accused of being "staidly traditional" (qtd. in Hyest 129). However, Spencer adamantly refused to alter her poetry for publication's sake, preferring to write her poetry and prose on ephemera. While some scholars have regarded Spencer's poetry as apolitical, raceless, and "staidly traditional," I am arguing that her poetics are inextricably linked to her lived experience as a Black woman and that she was acutely aware of the nuances of her positionality as a working-class Black woman. In other words, her writings do not simply reveal a feminist modernist poetics; they reveal careful meditations on Black womanhood as well.

Ecofeminists critique the conflation of "female" and "nature" because it "seeks to render the female subject mute and prone to masculinist exploitation and extraction" (Hicks 113).[4] For Black women in particular, nature can be a difficult symbol through which to mediate one's gender and sexuality because of its fraught colonial legacies.[5] Historian Jennifer L. Morgan explains that African women and their bodies were fraught with oppressive myths and stereotypes inscribed during slavery, ones that rendered them grotesque vessels of biological and economic reproduction (7). Just like the land, Black women and their bodies were marked as a natural resource to be exploited. Spencer embraces the conflation of "woman" and "nature," but she departs from the reductive notion of woman as "mother nature" and instead presents Black women's engagement and identification with the natural world as liberatory and as a means to transcend circumscribed notions of Black womanhood. Spencer's use of natural images can be read as a form of resistance through which she may assert her sexual autonomy and imagine greater freedom. Since what is natural is used to mobilize what is normal, her use of natural world symbols signals her attempt to destabilize heteronormativities and assert her right to define her gender and sexuality as she chooses.

In *Renegade Poetics: Black Aesthetics and Formal Innovation in African American Poetry,* Evie Shockley argues that Spencer's poetry reflects her unrelenting belief in equality and that her poetry mirrors her public efforts to effect change both in her personal life and larger society, "challeng[ing] us to further reconsider constructions of the New Negro Renaissance, recalling that Afro-modernity in the South was not predicated upon a wholesale removal from the natural world to an urban industrial one, but was signaled instead, perhaps, by the precious acquisition of a garden of one's own" (127, 144). Like Shockley's, my work continues the Black feminist scholarship of Gloria (Akasha) Hull, Deborah McDowell, Cheryl Wall, and Maureen Honey, who collectively reject the notion that New Negro Renaissance women's writing was apolitical, "feminine" poetry that did not address the nuances and politics of Black identity.

My analysis also explores the relationship between space and race—namely Black womanhood—and explicitly engages scholarship on Black feminist geographies. In *Demonic Grounds: Black Women and the Cartographies of Struggle*, Katherine McKittrick underscores the importance of the conceptualization and creation of space in understanding Black women's oppression, identifying it as a source of Black women's knowledge and domination. McKittrick explains, "I want to suggest that the category of black woman is intimately connected with the past and present spatial organization and that black femininity and black women's humanness are bound up in an ongoing geographic struggle" (xviii). By writing about her own intimate relationship with the natural world, Spencer is also reimagining and redefining the geographical dimensions of her lived experience. She is embarking on the project of space-making both within the confines of her own home and expanding the imaginative potentials of Black womanhood. In other words, she is literally and literarily creating new spaces and possibilities for Black women.

I use "space-making acts" to refer to the aesthetic practices Spencer employs to ensure that her undaunted Black female voice remains uncompromised in whatever form she chooses to express herself. Her critics found it difficult to hear a Black woman's voice through her sonnets, iambic pentameter, and musings about her garden. However, I am arguing that she critiques and simultaneously transforms traditional forms and stances into vehicles to articulate her Black feminist perspective. These space-making acts allow her to control her legibility because she sets forth the logics through which she wants to be recognized and understood. One example of Spencer's negotiation of space happens in the poem "Any Wife to Any Husband: A Derived Poem." This poem opens with seven poignant words: "This small garden is half my world" (Greene 186). What appears to be a statement of transparency is, in fact, a denial of access into the speaker's private life because she is boldly declaring a desire for privacy.[6] We are not told what the other half of her world is; this is left provocatively unclear. This omission sets a clear spatial boundary, so this opening line functions as a kind of velvet rope to let the reader know that the area beyond "this small garden" is inaccessible and unknowable. Though the speaker feigns transparency, she actually communicates, "I am *only* telling you what half my world is. You will not know what the other half is." This subtle linguistic directive is emblematic of Spencer's aesthetic space-making practice. Like her speaker, Spencer did not prioritize public legibility. That she was able to articulate the range of her imagination and humanity on *her* terms was enough. The key site for theoretical and artistic engagement for Spencer is the natural world, and her appropriation is a significant space-making act because she renders her Black female experience through symbols not intended for Black womanhood.

Situating Spencer's writing within the context of dominant narratives about the natural world is imperative because they serve as a critical point of departure for her work. In doing so, the magnitude of Spencer's intervention is highlighted, and we are able to identify the ways in which she rewrites and challenges the pervasive narratives. In *The Environmental Imagination,* Lawrence Buell traces the construction of the American environmental consciousness and environmental representation in literature and explains that the American environmental imaginary is hegemonic in that it has been based on texts by Anglo-American male writers such as Ralph Waldo Emerson and Henry David Thoreau and does not consider the perspectives of women and other American cultural groups (16).[7] After identifying "pastoralisms" in the works of writers such as Jean Toomer, Sterling Brown, and Zora Neale Hurston, Buell implies that the African American environmental imaginary will never compare to the Anglo-American's: "Although African American scholarship may never rediscover a neglected counterpart to Henry Thoreau, its geographical space has come to seem less city-oriented than it had seemed a generation ago notwithstanding the demographic facts" (18). Though Buell acknowledges the racist and sexist underpinnings of the American environmental imaginary, he seems to succumb to stereotypical rhetoric and suggests that the African American environmental imaginary, which he refers to as "African American pastoralism," lacks the sophistication and breadth of the Anglo-American imaginary because it lacks a counterpart to Thoreau. Buell's definition of "pastoral" is as follows: "For 'pastoral' has become almost synonymous with the idea of (re)turn to a less urbanized, more 'natural' state of existence.... Historically, pastoral has sometimes activated green consciousness, sometimes euphemized land appropriation. It may direct us toward the realm of physical nature, or it may abstract us from it. These I take to be the basic issues of ideology and representation posed by pastoral tradition" (31). Buell's statement about the nonexistence of a Black Thoreau illustrates the ways in which African Americans' connectedness to the natural world has been denied because implicit in his statement is the need for such a connectedness to be expressed, understood, and validated by the dominant society. Buell's text is certainly not representative of all writings on the Anglo-American imaginary, but it is against this type of narrative that Spencer's poetry intervenes. As Carolyn Finney explains, the privileging of perspectives from individuals like Thoreau has perpetuated a narrative that constructs African Americans as anti-environmental and alien to the natural world: "Prominent views of nature, while not unified, draw from the experiences of those in a position to influence and establish legitimacy for their ideas institutionally and culturally. Furthermore, these narratives, which contribute to the American environmental imaginary, are grounded in the values, beliefs, and attitudes of the individuals who construct them" (28).

Spencer's archive of natural world writings is a space-making oeuvre because it provides evidence of an existing Black environmental consciousness. Her poetry both provides an aperture through which we may see and analyze Black individuals' relationship to the environment and challenges dominant narratives that posit the natural world as a "white space." Both Spencer's daily life and poetry were intimately connected to her garden, and through her writings we see the significance of the natural world from the often-negated perspective of an African American individual. Thus, her body of work represents both a discursive and ideological reclamation of the natural world.[8]

I employ ecopoetics as an analytical framework that both encourages exploring the place of the natural world in Afro-diasporic women's writing and facilitates the method of close reading and textual analysis of natural world imagery in Black women's writing.[9] This introduction opened with an imperative from Georgia Douglas Johnson, and ecopoetics is a fitting framework for this analysis to reinforce that imperative. It is both descriptive and political because, as a combination of "ecology" and "poetics," it visually symbolizes the fusion and symbiosis Johnson calls for in her characterization of her dear friend and contains an implicit imperative not to separate "ecology" from "poetics." In *Female Pastoral,* Elizabeth Jane Harrison demonstrates how a nuanced examination of race and gender in such a male-centered genre as pastoral writing can shift traditional understandings and facilitate new readings of canonical texts (8–9). Harrison departs from traditional definitions of "pastoral" like Lawrence Buell's, which center white, male authors, and argues that there is a "female pastoral" genre that "becomes, unlike the male tradition, a liberating, visionary genre rather than a reactionary or critical one" (11). Centering race, gender, and sexuality, Harrison is able to delineate the ways in which female authors "re-vision" pastoral writing (11). Though her analysis is not rooted in Black women's materiality, Harrison's attention to race and gender enables her to notice the specificities of Black women's pastoral writing: "For black women authors in this new tradition, nature is an overriding force that must be respected rather than overcome or tamed as it is in the white version" (11). Like Harrison's interrogation of pastoral writing, my study of ecopoetics analyzes how Black women "re-vision" natural world writing.

As a study that foregrounds "poetic artifice as a manifestation of [human] interrelation with the rest of nature" (Knickerbocker 159), ecopoetics is not new to the field of literary criticism; however, its relevance and application to Black women's writing has been largely uninterrogated.[10] My proposed expansion of ecopoetics is heavily indebted to and extends Katherine McKittrick's framework of analyzing the cartographies of Black women's struggles and L. H. Stallings's theory of *funky erotixxx* that "problematize[s] the erotic and what it means to be human" (Stallings xv). Stallings reminds us that the public sphere does not have to be the sole realm through which Black women mediate their sex and theorize their gender and sexuality (150). Ecopoetics provides a window into Black women's interiors and reveals how Black women articulate and negotiate their sexuality and gender identities beyond the public sphere. This interior articulation is akin to Kevin Quashie's conceptualization of "quiet": "Quiet is the expressiveness of the inner life, unable to be expressed fully but nonetheless articulate and informing one's humanity. As a concept, it helps us explore black subjectivity from beyond the boundaries of public expressiveness" (24). Like the aforementioned authors' frameworks, ecopoetics invites us to think about Black women's materiality and subjectivity in new ways, reveals how central and inextricably linked the natural world is to Black women's theorizing, and asks, *What happens when Black women mediate their sexuality and gender through the natural world?*

Black artists' attention to the natural world reveals the important and uninvestigated connections between literary ecocriticism and representations of trauma in Black literature. In Billie Holiday's "Strange Fruit," she sings of "Black bodies swinging in the southern breeze/Strange fruit hanging from the poplar trees."[11] In *Beloved,* Sethe's "Chokecherry tree" scar on her back is a reminder of the physical abuse she endured during enslavement. The photojournalism project *Without Sanctuary* is a visual testament to the public celebration of lynching and is filled with images of brutally murdered African Americans hanging from trees.[12] These are only a few examples of the ways in which trees represent sites of trauma within African American literature and history. Paul Outka's important work *Race and Nature from Transcendentalism to the Harlem Renaissance* is among the first to bridge the fields of critical race studies and ecocriticism and illustrates that "nature is a human, ideological construction that generally reflects the political, cultural, and economic needs of the viewer" (54).

Grounded in theories of sublimity and trauma, Outka traces the origins of a racialized nature to the Romantic sublime and aptly highlights how "sublime experience functioned in the formation of race" (201). Given this association with trauma, ecocriticism and ecopoetics may seem like unlikely pairings for Black women's writings.

Foregrounding Black women's ecological materialities is necessary because it is one of the many ways Black women theorize their lived experiences; to negate it risks lobotomizing Black women's theoretical interventions, expressiveness, and humanity. My study of ecopoetics analyzes how Black women "re-vision"[13] natural world writing and challenges the deliberate, conscious exclusion of Black writing from environmental literary criticism, which has racialized the natural world as a white space, and refutes stereotypes of Black environmental apathy. Such an analysis is imperative to bear witness to the ways Black women writers resist the designation, "De nigger woman is de mule uh de world" (Hurston, *Their Eyes* 14) and undermine the colonial legacies that render them perpetually exploitable. I suggest that Black women writers' use of natural imagery is a discursive strategy through which they can imagine greater geographic possibilities for Black women; they are articulating both their womanhood and humanity. When we consider the geographical dimensions of their experiences, we see that they are also engaging in a theorizing of space, a theorizing, Barbara Christian contends, that is innate to Black women's writing (68). I argue that their use of natural imagery is powerful symbolism through which they map their own contours of a self-fashioned womanhood and implicitly invite other Black women to do the same. In doing so, they transcend oppressive, circumscribed notions of womanhood. Their use of natural images is a form of claims-making through which they may assert their sexual autonomy and both articulate and reimagine their race and gender. This claims-making is a necessary self-representation strategy because, as Carla L. Peterson explains, bodies are "never divorced from perception and interpretation," and Black womanhood and Black women's bodies, in particular, bear a historical legacy of "simultaneous masculinization and femininization . . . which was consequently perceived as grotesque" ("Foreword" ix–xi).

I depart from analyzing Black environmental engagement through the lens of trauma and instead position the natural world as a generative, liberatory space. This alternative reading is in line with current critiques within ecocriticism that call for an engagement with texts by persons of color and women. Critics Karla Armbruster and Kathleen R. Wallace argue that an ecocriticism that exclusively focuses on white, male-authored texts perpetuates harmful misconceptions that depict the natural world as "untrammeled American wilderness" (7). Such misconceptions, Kimberly N. Ruffin contends, lead to the understanding of the natural world as an inherently white, male space and create the ideological breeding ground for such acts of environmental racism as the August 2006 Jena Six case in which Black high school students in central Louisiana were the targets of racist threats for sitting under "the white tree" (1). In *Black on Earth,* Ruffin foregrounds her ecocritical readings of African American literary texts with an analysis of the incident involving the Jena Six teenagers to underscore the contemporary relevance of ecocriticism and to delineate how Black individuals exist as "ecological pariahs" and "environmental others" (2, 16). Ruffin argues, "Indeed, if we are to transform the figurative and actual white trees of ecological exclusion, we must expand ecocritical language to befit a more representative imaginative landscape" (13). As a theory that explores the relationship between humans and nature, ecopoetics pushes against monolithic visions of the natural world because it necessitates a consideration of all intersecting identities that inform human experiences. As previously noted, articulating notions of Black womanhood and sexuality through the natural world can be challenging because of colonial legacies. With Black women's writings, ecopoetics facilitates readings that move beyond trauma and asks us to interrogate the ways Black women writers "re-vision" the environment to articulate their race, gender, sexuality, and humanity.

I employ ecopoetics to consider how Spencer's use of natural world imagery allows her to destabilize and question prescriptive notions of normative Black womanhood and sexuality. Specifically, I am arguing that it yields four contributions: *first,* it enables readers to bear witness to the Black environmental imaginary, which, as noted above, has been an overlooked site of inquiry in ecocritical studies. *Second,* it shifts contemporary ecocritical discourses by centering Black women's fictions and exploring the place of the natural world and ecological materialities in Black women's literature. *Third,* it allows one to engage in discourses of Blackness and non-normative sexuality, further expanding the field of ecocriticism. *Fourth,* it facilitates comparative, diasporic analyses without eliding differences. My research is broadly governed by the following overarching questions: What is Anne Spencer's conception of "natural" and "nature"? What does nature tell us about non-normative erotics, affect, and intimacies in her writing? What does this focus on non-normativity mean for the questions of representation of Black womanhood I engage? How does it impact conceptions of space?

Do Not Separate Her from Her Garden is organized into four chapters that highlight specific aspects of Spencer's poetics and her critical environmental consciousness. Chapter 1, "'Leventy-Leven Bits Stuck in As Many Different Places': Anne Spencer's Eccentricity," is an analysis and close reading of Anne Spencer's space-making acts. This chapter considers her unpublished works and the Papers of Anne Spencer and the Spencer Family as a whole. I conduct close readings of her poetry and prose, and I also perform close readings of the visual representations of her writing. To engage with the Papers of Anne Spencer and the Spencer Family, one must abandon conventional notions of time, space, and logic and completely surrender to the world she created. Spencer literally wrote on anything and about anything. Equally important as *what* Spencer wrote is *how* Spencer wrote, so this chapter considers the myriad objects she transformed into her writings and spaces for her poems. The literal space-making she performed in her garden is mirrored in the way she wrote her poetry. Most of Spencer's prose writings are undated and untitled, and I argue that Spencer's affinity for writing poetry on ephemera is a space-making strategy that allows her to manipulate both time and space (and maintain control), as the reader must surrender to her direction. Through her transformation of ephemeral objects into canvasses for her poems, Spencer also made space for herself, one that suited her more than the coercive, prescriptive world of publishing.

Though a brilliant, prolific writer and theorist, Spencer loathed publication and wrote simply for the sake of writing. Publication stifled her, and she only submitted to journals at the urging of such friends as James Weldon Johnson and W. E. B. Du Bois. Spencer's writings reveal that though she was not actively writing, she was contributing to New Negro Renaissance culture. However, her frequent interaction and correspondence with fellow New Negro artists positions her at the center of the New Negro Renaissance and U.S. literary modernism more generally. Spencer's prolific writings also call into question publication as the sole measure of one's contribution to and involvement in a literary movement. One of the limitations of Spencer's archive is the absence of a nuanced account of the inner workings of her literary salon during the period after World War I through the 1920s. She indeed entertained and corresponded with such intellectuals as W. E. B. Du Bois and such fellow New Negro Movement writers as Georgia Douglas Johnson and Langston Hughes in her Lynchburg, Virginia, home. Her correspondence not only reveals her presence as a New Negro Renaissance artist but demonstrates that, though she was not actively publishing new creative pieces, she was a part of the nexus of artists and thinkers who were imagining new possibilities and potential for Black individuals. This chapter exposes the challenges of working within a Black woman's archive, as outlined by Ula Taylor, and ultimately seeks to work both within and against the limitations of the archive and "disrupt those canonical discourses that have too often rendered African American women invisible" (Taylor 195).

The second chapter, "'This Small Garden Is Half My World': Anne Spencer's Ecopoetics," provides an in-depth analysis of Spencer's critical environmental consciousness and traces the development of her ecopoetics. It positions Spencer's garden as both essential to her creative work and as a restorative space vital to her existence. Ultimately, this chapter is an analysis of Spencer's gender politics, her meditations on Black womanhood, and her articulation of these mediations using the language and symbolism of the natural world. The posthumously published poems "[Earth, I thank you]," "Any Wife to Any Husband," and "He Said" are analyzed, as both the natural world and notions of Black womanhood are the central themes. In these "nature poems," Spencer articulates a profound sense of desire for and connectedness to the natural world, and it becomes particularly clear that for Spencer her garden was vital source of inspiration for her writing and life.

Anne Spencer was a deeply spiritual individual, and my third chapter, "'God Never Planted a Garden': Anne Spencer's Ecotheology," illustrates that even her spiritual life could not be separated from her love of nature. In this chapter I argue that nature served as a kind of mediator in her spiritual life, so she utilizes ecological analogies to articulate meditations on such topics as love, matrimony, motherhood, parenting, religion, and God. Nature functions as the prism through which she views herself and the various aspects of her life. She views virtually everything in relation to the natural world, and this chapter demonstrates how her deep connectedness to the natural world undergirded her beliefs. This chapter seeks to answer precisely how Spencer conceives of the natural world and considers the various biblical and philosophical traditions she utilizes to inform her ideologies.

In the fourth chapter, "'I Proudly Love Being a Negro Woman': Anne Spencer's 'Natural' Means of Expression," I argue that Spencer's modernism is revealed and best understood when juxtaposed with her gender politics and her environmental consciousness. As a Black woman-poet-mother-wife-civil-rights-and-community-activist-intellectual-librarian-environmentalist, Anne Spencer employs this emergent, experimental form of modernism to articulate the breadth of her identity and politics and presents a vision of Black womanhood that undermines the ideologies espoused in Elise Johnson McDougald's essay "The Task of Negro Womanhood." The most modern aspect of Spencer's poetry is the way she deploys her environmental consciousness to both redefine and critique traditional notions of womanhood; therefore, just as her feminism necessitated her modernism, so did her environmentalism. Spencer's concern with Black women's right to happiness is seen through her use of natural world symbols, and it is perhaps this affinity for modernism and the natural world that caused some critics to deem her work unconventional.

My fifth and final chapter, "Do Not Separate Them from Their Gardens: Black Women's Writings and Ecopoetics," restates my central claims about Spencer and demonstrates that there is a rich legacy of natural world writing in Black women's literature. Scenes from Zora Neale Hurston's *Their Eyes Were Watching God*, Alice Walker's *The Color Purple*, and Dionne Brand's *In Another Place, Not Here* illustrate the rich legacy of Black women's natural world writings and underscore how readings of Black women's literature may be enhanced when we consider their ecological materialities. By engaging Hurston's and Walker's canonical novels and Brand's more recent text, the uninvestigated presences of ecofeminist engagement with Black women's writings are illuminated and call attention to contemporary texts that bring that legacy forward. I draw on Tiffany Ruby Patterson and Robin D. G. Kelley's definition of diaspora in "Unfinished Migrations: Reflections on the African Diaspora and the Making of the Modern World" as both "a process and a condition" and heed their critique of diasporic analyses that tend to elide differences (20). Using an ecoliterary lens facilitates an attention to nuance and difference and enables readers to discuss the discursive strategies through which Afro-diasporic women writers create the contours of their own visions of womanhood. Exploring the connections between the natural world symbolisms and Black womanhood allows readers to identify a common ground between Afro-diasporic women's writings in a way that does not elide difference.

The book's coda, "If People Were Like Flowers," restates this work's central claims about Anne Spencer and demonstrates that there is a rich legacy of natural world writing in Black women's literature and argues that an ecoliterary lens enables readers to analyze and bear witness to the fact that natural world writing is a part of Black women's theoretical savviness and creativity. Here, I discuss the larger implications of this single-author study and position ecocritical readings and ecopoetics as legitimate sites for Black feminist engagement and queer studies and critique traditional ecocriticism's failure to consider the intersections of race, sexuality, and gender.

Georgia Douglas Johnson's implicit imperative that opens this introduction is a retrospective statement that honors and respects the way Spencer articulates herself. I say that her statement is retrospective because when she writes this letter, it is approximately thirty years after the height of New Negro Renaissance artistic production and well after the era in which Spencer published. In these pages, I am honoring Anne Spencer's legacy as a gifted writer and audacious Black woman who dared to create and define her world on her terms. Ultimately, this work is an act of obeisance in which I do not separate Spencer from her garden. Most importantly, this book is an expression of gratitude. Working with Spencer's poetry and experiencing her archive have taught me to be retrospective when listening to Black women's poetics. Spencer has taught me that not only should I not separate her from her garden, but I also should not separate Black women writers from their gardens—in whatever forms they may take. Thank you, Annie Bethel Scales Spencer.[14] Amen.

1

"'Leventy-Leven Bits Stuck in As Many Different Places"

Anne Spencer's Eccentricity

"I have nothing new finished. But there are 'leventy-leven bits stuck in as many different places that promise something if I ever get at them."[1] Anne Spencer penned these words in a drafted letter to her close friend and fellow writer and poet James Weldon Johnson. Fittingly, she wrote this note on the back of a letter from James Weldon Johnson, who regularly requested poetry from her and encouraged her to keep writing. This statement highlights Spencer's relationship to her writing and the uniqueness of her archive. For Spencer, writing was an infinite process, and her archive is a small glimpse into the "different places" she saw fit to house her writing. Anne Spencer was audaciously odd, eccentric, and weird, and her archive at the University of Virginia is a celebration of her eccentricity. To engage with the Papers of Anne Spencer and the Spencer Family, one must abandon conventional notions of time, space, and logic, and completely surrender to the world she created. Spencer literally wrote *on* everything and *about* everything. And when I say that Spencer wrote on everything, I am referring to the astonishing collection of ephemeral objects she transformed into canvasses for her writing. So equally important as *what* Spencer wrote is *how* Spencer wrote. Such notable examples of the places she made space for her poems include her husband Edward's accounting ledgers, and the top of a shoe box. This chapter considers the myriad objects she transformed into her writings and spaces for her poems.[2] J. Lee Greene took note of Spencer's unconventional writing process and affinity for ephemera, highlighting that her writing was personally edifying: "Sometimes she would awake in the middle of the night and write something, some-where—a 'habit' she never was able to break. Even some of the books in her library have their blank pages filled with lines of poetry, critical evaluations of or responses to ideas in the books, or 'just thoughts.' She remarked that she always had written primarily for her own enjoyment and not for pub-lication or praise" (50). Greene also recalls an anecdote Spencer shared in which she spontaneously penned the poem "Dunbar" in an effort to teach her students about the fundamentals of poetry and suggests that Spencer's desire to expose children to literature may explain the some of the drafts of verses and stories seen in her archive (86).

After visiting her archive at the University of Virginia, I was struck by two things: first, from a visual standpoint her archive is a beautifully over-whelming sensory experience that consists of prose and poetry written on carefully chosen surfaces on topics ranging from theology and slavery to motherhood and politics. Her archive is both visually overwhelming and intellectually provocative. The second aspect that intrigued me is that her connection to the natural world was articulated everywhere, not just in her poetry. It was not just a hobby. Gardening indeed was a creative outlet for Spencer, but much more than that. She constructed her sense of being around and through the natural world. Chapters 2 and 4 of this book directly engage Spencer's connection to and theorizing of the natural world, but I invoke her garden here to suggest that in the same way Spen-cer's garden was carefully designed, so was her archive. The architectural nature of her archive indicates that Spencer was also concerned with its materiality. Spencer's unorthodox archive of unpublished, undated poems and prose written on ephemera and other materials is a rich text and space-making act in itself, and I read it as a beautiful illustration of the audacious eccentricity she embodied in her daily life. This chapter also considers the visual eccentricity and materiality of her archive. Like her garden, Spen-cer's archive produces a sensory experience. Through her transformation of ephemeral objects into canvasses for her writings, Spencer also made space for herself, a space that suited her more than the coercive, prescrip-tive world of publishing. Space-making is an act of making one's self legible. Through her eccentric performance, Spencer controlled her legibility while being odd and unusual.

For Spencer, writing was a process devoid of circumscribed beginnings and endings; it existed along a continuum for her and was a process that was vital to her existence. This chapter argues that the literal space-making she performed in her garden is mirrored in the way she wrote her poetry. I use "space-making acts" to refer to the aesthetic choices Spencer makes in her writing to ensure that her unapologetically Black female voice remained uncompromised in whatever form she chose to express herself. This space-making strategy allows her to manipulate time and space and to control her legibility because the reader must surrender to *her* direction; *she* sets forth the logics through which she wants to be recognized and understood. The unconventionality of a Black woman's archive is central to both this book and this chapter. Spencer's institutional archive and her body of work are *new* archives in that they have received minimal engagement, so are therefore relatively *new* to Black women's literary studies.[3] Spencer's work also introduces Black women's natural world writings as an unexplored archive and as a legitimate site of Black feminist epistemology; therefore, Anne Spencer's physical, institutional archive functions as a doorway to understand the many ways Black women theorize and produce knowledge.

I use the word "eccentric" to describe Spencer because she was audaciously odd and weird. She was an untypical Black woman, whose daily routine consisted of rising at 11:00 a.m., bathing for one hour, followed by brushing her hair for two hours, and spending the afternoon and evening gardening and writing until about 2:00 a.m. In my discussion of eccentricity, I draw upon Carla L. Peterson's foreword to *Recovering the Black Female Body: Self-Representations by African American Women* (2001) and Francesca T. Royster's *Sounding Like a No-No: Queer Sounds & Eccentric Acts in the Post-Soul Era* (2013). Peterson introduces the concept of eccentricity as a subversive self-representation strategy Black women writers used as a means to appropriate and reclaim the label of "eccentricity" thrust upon them and their bodies. Pointing to the double entendre in the word, Peterson defines it as "an axis not centrally placed (according to the dominant system), whereas the second extends the notion of off-centeredness to suggest freedom of movement stemming from the lack of central control and hence new possibilities of difference conceived as empowering oddness" (xi–xii). Royster extends Peterson's definition and includes individuals and acts that deviate from normative channels of legibility: "not only out of the ordinary or unconventional performances but also those that are ambiguous, uncanny, or difficult to read. . . . Through acts of spectacular creativity, the eccentric joins forces with the 'queer,' 'freak,' and 'pervert' to see around corners, push the edges of the present to create a language not yet recognized: new sounds, new dances, new configurations of self—the makings of a black utopia" (8). Royster's study of eccentricity is rooted in the late twentieth and early twenty-first centuries (during the Soul and post-Soul eras).[4] I affirm Royster's analysis and argue that Spencer is a pre-Soul of iteration of Black eccentricity, one that is also rooted in a desire for freedom—the freedom to be untypical. Spencer's eccentricity offers a new way to think about Black womanhood "being-ness" during the New Negro Renaissance.[5]

This chapter and this work in its totality are acutely aware of the nuances and challenges of working within a Black woman's archive, challenges that Darlene Clarke Hine and Ula Taylor delineate in their essays about the challenges of writing Black women's histories.[6] In writing this chapter, I feel moved to note that such a formal, institutional collection is not something that Anne Spencer would have desired. Spencer's "'leventy-leven bits stuck in as many different places" were perfect to her. Public legibility was not a priority to Spencer—controlling it was—so the clandestine nature of her archive was another means through which she could control her legibility. While I heed Taylor's imperative that scholars of Black women's studies must "disrupt those canonical discourses that have too often rendered African American women invisible" (195), I also seek to honor the "culture of dissemblance" (Hine 380) that Spencer may have adopted as a means to shield herself from the vulnerability she experienced as a southern Black woman at the mercy of Jane Crow.[7]

With regard to Spencer's archive, I am informed by Ann Cvetkovich's *An Archive of Feelings* and her construction of a lesbian and gay archive of trauma. Though not rooted in trauma, Spencer's archive is indeed unorthodox, but as Cvetkovich argues, such ephemera and "personal collections of objects stand alongside the documents of the dominant culture in order to offer alternative forms of knowledge" (8). Anne Spencer's archive is a testament to her eccentricity. To the outside world, Spencer's archive and writing process do not "make sense"—and, here, I use the idiom to denote a lack of reason or comprehension. However, her archive indeed does "make sense" in that it produces a powerful sensory experience. Spencer's archive is a physical, sensory experience; it must be *touched,* and it must be *felt.* She was rooted in her eccentricity, and her eccentricity was dangerous and daring, especially considering her positionality as a southern Black woman living under the watchful eyes of Jim Crow. Ultimately, this chapter seeks to honor Spencer's archive and archive-making as legitimate forms of knowledge and celebrate her audacity to be eccentric. In doing so, I highlight that Spencer was bold and daring enough to articulate her Black womanhood in whatever form she chose, so her unapologetically Black female voice remained uncompromised. Signaling Taylor, Hine, and Cvetkovich is my way of thinking about materiality while at the same time thinking about public versus private and how Black women, like Spencer, worked to privilege their right to discretion and privacy.

I want to return to the quote that opens this chapter and analyze the "'leventy-leven bits stuck in as many different places" because it signals Spencer's own archiving process, which is emblematic of her eccentricity and how beautifully she controlled her legibility even in the most public of spaces. Spencer's use of "'leventy-leven" could easily be misinterpreted as a typographical error to those unfamiliar with African American Vernacular English, as it is akin to such exaggerative numerical idioms as "fifty-'leven." This playful quantifying, however, is an example of her improvisational practice and inventiveness because Spencer is making up numbers and creating a language to count her "manyness." As she signals "manyness" Spencer also establishes her autonomy and reveals that she will articulate herself on her own terms—even if it means inventing a new language through which to express herself. In doing so, Spencer is invoking and insisting upon her uncontainability.

When Spencer lived in her home, most of her writings were kept in boxes or loose-leafed pages on her staircase. This staircase was a kind of "filing cabinet" for Spencer, and she left a very narrow walkway for individuals to travel up and down the stairs. In spite of the seeming disorganization, Spencer knew exactly where everything was.[8] Though humor was likely intended in Spencer's note to Johnson, her specificity about the "'leventy-leven bits stuck in as many different places" reveals that that her collection of "bits of paper" was carefully and deliberately constructed. There is something very public yet very private about her staircase-filing cabinet that mirrors her relationship to her writing and her performance as a Black woman. Spencer's staircase of writings highlights the dissonance between what she visually shares and what she withholds and are what I call *public displays of privacy*. I use this term to describe how Spencer sets boundaries and denies access to her interior. Instead of wearing a "mask that grins and lies" (Dunbar, "We Wear the Mask" 1), Spencer insists on her right to have and protect her privacy. What is most compelling and provocative about her public displays of privacy is what Spencer chooses not to share or display.

For instance, the staircase is located very prominently in the Spencer home and provides the only access to the bedrooms and bathroom. Any resident or guest of Spencer's—and she entertained regularly—would have been forced to see her boxes, and they would have had no other choice but to literally tiptoe around her writings to gain access to the home's sole

bathroom. Though her writings were on display, they were private and protected from the public because only Spencer knew the contents of each box
and each page. To anyone except for Spencer, this collection of writings was
probably evidence of her aversion for domestic tasks and the household
unkemptness for which she was known (Greene 45–46). However, to Spencer, these writings—these "bits"—were pieces of her. In her correspondence
to James Weldon Johnson, she often referred to her writing very intimately
as her "private thoughts" (Greene 66), and of her poetry she writes, "I don't
negate my poems—they are me in the years here [;] they are my conversation
with myself."[9] The preservation of her work in *her* unconventional way is just
as important as the content of her poems because her poems were parts of
her; it was also an act of self-preservation. The boxes on the staircase are a
bold statement that Spencer's writing is autonomously hers and hers alone.

Like her writings, there were parts of Spencer that were inaccessible.
When we consider the implications of the parts of her strewn about her
home within the context of the Jim Crow South, her eccentricity is quite
dangerous. During a time in which Black bodies were policed and told
which spaces they could and could not occupy, Spencer embarked on
making space for herself and her writing. These boxes are a physical manifestation of how Spencer was moving freely and literally creating space
for herself and her ideas. Though the "clutter" on her staircase may seem
insignificant, we must remember that Spencer's home served as one of
the three major literary salons during the New Negro Renaissance, and
she entertained guests, both Black and white, on a regular basis.[10] Anyone
who entered her home would have had to physically engage with her writings and carefully tiptoe around them. Her archive was a physical, material experience that one had to confront. Spencer not only creates space
for herself though her archiving, but she *transforms* and *shifts* space. One
would literally have to move around her work, not the other way around,
which, in a place like Lynchburg, Virginia, is a profoundly atypical act of
deference extended toward a Black woman. The hypervisibility and sensory
nature of her archive is an intentional statement of controlled legibility.
The Spencer home is quite spacious, objectively speaking, and contains
multiple guest rooms and an attic. Spencer also had her writing cottage,
Edankraal, located in her garden, which she did utilize to store some—but
not all—of her writing. In other words, Spencer could have utilized other
spaces to situate her archive, but its location suggests that Spencer desired
both visibility and concealment, publicity and privacy. As she does in her
poetry, Spencer sets forth the logics through which she is to be understood

and engaged. These boxes are not mere clutter; they are constructions of a Black woman's world.

In this way, Spencer's home functioned as a gallery and as a form of publication for her writings, one that suited her more than the coercive realm of publication. Spencer's reluctance to publish her writing echoes her aversion toward objectification, containment, and commodification. What I mean by that is that Spencer deliberately moved away from utilitarian motives and thinking. Spencer, herself, was very anxious about being consumed and rarely published her poetry. Her archive is filled with letters from such friends and contemporaries as W. E. B. Du Bois and James Weldon Johnson, who repeatedly urged her to submit her writing for publication (Greene 65). Spencer was quite sensitive to editorial comments about her poetry and public scrutiny of her writing. One notable example of this is her response to an offer, following the death of James Weldon Johnson, to have her correspondence appear in a special collection at Yale. Spencer insisted that she be able to edit the correspondence first: "I wouldn't wish my letters, if any, to go into the collection unless I edited them: I'm afraid . . . surely, that in those days I was ingenuous enough to try to appear intellectual without being intelligent" (qtd. in Greene 66). I do not intend to suggest that Spencer was insecure or lacked confidence in her writing. However, Greene notes that she expressed a "yearning for approval and success" (61). Spencer was also very acutely aware of her positionality as a Black woman in her published writing and felt the need to censor herself to avoid controversy.[11] Thus, the boxes on her staircase were not only a form of publication for Spencer; they also constituted a space, a liminal area, in which she did not have to be censored.

There is something avant-garde about Spencer's preferred method of displaying her writings because it forces us to expand our understanding of what publication entails; it forces us, as readers, to think differently about what publication means. And, indeed, Spencer's writing practice forced others to think differently as well, not only because they had to literally move around her work but also because she rarely acquiesced to requests to publish it for others. Spencer's home-gallery functions not only as a space where she can publish her writings on her own terms but also as a space through which Spencer can articulate her nonutilitarian stance. Indeed, her writing is on display; however, like the fruit trees and flowers in her garden, it is not for consumption. Thus, she establishes an "art for art's sake" mode of thinking that undermines the utilitarian conflation of writing and print publication. That she establishes her home as an alternative publication space calls into question print publication as the sole measure of participation (and success) during the New Negro Renaissance period (and beyond) and also underscores the oft-overlooked labor that women artists performed during this period.[12] She creates a space in which just being and becoming are enough.

Spencer masterfully and strategically plays with signification.[13] Though she specularizes herself through her work, she is also cleverly concealed and veiled. Spencer's ability to move between hypervisibility and covering evokes Annie Anlin Cheng's discussion of Josephine Baker's ability to manipulate what her body signified even when she was performing nude: "Baker constantly gives us surface rather than body. Even in her most 'embodied' dances it can be argued that it is her kinesthetic energy rather than her corporeal presence that transmits" (63). In the same way that Baker is able to shift signification away from her hypervisible, denuded body, Anne Spencer's boxes of writings perform the same illusory work. Like Baker's bare skin, Spencer's boxes of writings appear to transmit a legible presence, but, in reality, they are surfaces.

What is remarkable about Spencer's brand of eccentricity is that it feigns transparency, publicity, and full disclosure. The boxes were in plain sight and yet simultaneously invisible and inaccessible. Although they were visible and palpable, Spencer would have to explain *what* they are. This delicate dance of balancing the public and private is indeed masterfully clever, but recall that writing was a practice that sustained Spencer. As previously noted, Spencer's manuscripts are written on various ephemera. I deliberately refer to her "fragmentary" writing as manuscripts and not "drafts" or "incomplete writings" to honor her logics and writing process. Although chapter 4 of this work discusses Spencer's modernist techniques, here I want to note that these fragmentary writings might also be a modernist assertion of fragmentation in the world embodied in her writing process and presentation. In *In Search of Our Mothers' Gardens* Alice Walker reminds us of the "creative spirit that the black woman has inherited" (239) and of the overlooked artistry in Black women's lived experiences. Spencer's writing and archiving processes are such examples of the "creative spirit" Walker mentions and serve as a reminder that art and poetry can exist and be created beyond the print form and can even take the form of boxes on staircase.

The same type of barrier that Spencer created physically through her boxes, she also created linguistically, and this is beautifully illustrated in the opening quote: "I have nothing new finished. But there are 'leventy-leven bits stuck in as many different places that promise something if I ever get at them." To further unpack Spencer's prose, we must note that it is likely she is writing this letter in response to Johnson's request for additional poetry. But rather than say what could be said relatively simply—"I have nothing to submit for publication at this time" or "I am not interested in publishing my writings"—Spencer, instead, responds in a very complicated manner. I want to move through this statement slowly and chronologically and analyze Spencer's performative coyness and deflection because, though it is very subtle, her demand for privacy is masterful. Spencer opens with a terse independent clause: "I have nothing new finished." There is an elegant hesitancy in this clause: Notice that Spencer does not simply say she has "nothing." Instead, she hints that she indeed has been writing by saying she has "nothing new." However, it is unclear what she means by "new," as that could denote writing that is "recent," "original," "groundbreaking," or "individual." Her use of "finished" is also strategic. Recall that Johnson was both Spencer's dear friend and her trusted editor, so this letter functions as both friendly correspondence and an attempt to evade Johnson's incessant requests for Spencer to submit more poems for publication. Spencer spent most of her life declining her friends' requests to submit her writing for publication. Most notably, Johnson playfully threatened to "beat" her, and her foray into publishing ceased with Johnson's death in 1938 (qtd. in Greene 65). Similarly, in a letter dated December 19, 1927, W. E. B. Du Bois wrote that he would resort to printing her correspondence if Spencer did not send him any new poems.[14] In saying that she has "nothing new finished," Spencer indeed acknowledges the metrics of the publishing world and appears to be volunteering the information that Johnson is requesting. However, this statement is also Spencer's way of preserving her unique archiving and writing processes. She does not simply say that she has "nothing." Through her use of "nothing new," she affirms her own writing process, which was one of careful revising that she continued until her death. Though she acknowledges Johnson's (and print publication's) metrics, she is ultimately making a statement about what *she* values.

Notice that Spencer does not disclose what she *does* have. Her use of "new" and "finished" implies that she is making a comparative statement—though not a hierarchical one—about the writings that she does have, namely that they are "not new" and "not finished." That she hints at her "not new," "not finished" writing and does not name it explicitly, underscores that she desires privacy for her writings and also enables her to subtly communicate her own value system. In other words, she communicates that her fragmentary manuscripts may not be acceptable for print publication, but they have meaning and value to her. Thus, this brief independent clause is imbued with an affirmation that says, "I write for myself; my writings are my own." As a frequent guest of her home, Johnson was probably aware of her unique archiving, so there is also a way in which this statement reiterates that the boxes on her staircase are off-limits to him and the outside world.

The second independent clause begins with the conjunction "but" and deceptively suggests that Spencer is preparing to contradict or retract her previous statement. Instead, she offers a statement fraught with ambiguity: "But there are 'leventy-leven bits stuck in as many different places that promise something if I ever get at them." Though this clause would cause a frequent house guest, like Johnson, to conjure specific images of her staircase, Spencer shifts to using the passive voice as if to distance herself from ownership of the "'leventy-leven bits." Surely, Spencer is referencing her own writing. However, the passivity and imprecision of "But there are" give her writing an ethereal, expansive quality, one that is affirmed by her use of "stuck in as many different places." Spencer shifts from the active voice and literally removes herself from subjectivity and employs the passive voice, creating further ambiguity and forcing the reader to ask such questions as, *To whom do the "bits" belong?* and *Who stuck the bits in so many different places?*

The location of "as many different places" she provides is simultaneously specific yet abstruse, and, once again, she is insisting upon her "manyness." She also renames her manuscripts as "bits," and this renaming mirrors her invention of "'leventy-leven" because "bits" also signals her inventiveness and creativity. While "bits" could certainly refer to her writings, it could also refer to the various ephemera upon which she wrote. Thus, one must do a considerable amount of inferring and speculation to decipher what Spencer means here, and one is forced to assume that Spencer is referring to writings and specifically her writings, at that. Notice what Spencer says about the "'leventy-leven bits": that they "promise something if I ever get at them." "They" (the bits) is the subject of the verb "promise," so Spencer is deferring to her writings and saying that *they*, not she, promise something. In other words, she does not have to promise anything. Spencer anthropomorphizes her writing and again seems to distance herself from her writing, her art. This is a curious linguistic gesture that could certainly be attributed to Spencer's nonchalance and coyness. But we must recall her use of "'leventy-leven" as a metonym for her "manyness." In distancing herself from her art, Spencer is not necessarily denying herself authorial credit, but rather she is carefully and deliberately insisting upon her multiplicity by not conflating herself with her writing. While, indeed, her writing is a part of her, her writing is *not* her, and she is not *just* her writing. The progression of "promise something if" are a linguistic unraveling, as Spencer moves from definitive to conditional. The sturdiness of "promise" is immediately undermined and questioned by the ambiguity of the "something." Certainly, this "something" could signal poems not yet written, but Spencer leaves this vague. This equivocal promise is conditional and hinges on Spencer, and she is careful to provide the caveat "if I ever get at them," underscoring, once again, that she has a right to (and will) privilege her right to discretion and privacy.

This statement is also a reflection of how Spencer's "garden, verse, and sure philosophy" are inextricably linked. We may read the "bits" in so many different places and the boxes on her staircase as a kind of gardening, and here I want to remind us that gardening is also defined as "the work or art of a gardener" and is not limited to the actual act of cultivating or tending to a physical garden space ("gardening"). Because Spencer has literally planted her writings in specific, albeit undisclosed, places, and they require cultivation—she must "get at them" so they can yield the promised something. There is a relationship of nurturing, cultivating, and tending to that is being evoked here. This was the way her garden of writings had to grow.

What is most compelling about this quote is that it is from a *drafted* letter, so it is possible that Spencer never sent a finished draft and that she never intended to send a finished draft. One of the unique characteristics of Spencer's archive is that it is filled with drafted letters and responses to individuals, organizations, and current events most of which were never sent. This act of writing letters without the intention of sending them might seem peculiar, but we must recall that Spencer very deliberately and carefully moved away from utilitarian motives and thinking in relation to her writing. Though the drafted letter is addressed to Johnson, there is a way in which we can think of this drafted letter to herself and for herself. In other words, if we remove Johnson as the intended recipient, this statement becomes an affirmation reminding her that writing and being of writing is enough. Indeed, Johnson is the intended recipient, but, ultimately, this quote affirms that she does not have to write *for* Johnson. It serves as a reminder that she does not have to write for, or write to, that writing and being of writing is enough. The above quote is simple prose, but it is carefully written and is rich with insight into Spencer's meditations on her relationship to her writing. The scholars who have engaged with the Papers of Anne Spencer and the Spencer Family have primarily consulted the manuscripts that are more conventional in appearance. However, as demonstrated with the above quote, though the visual representation and materiality of Spencer's writing may differ between her published writings and unpublished, undated manuscripts, Spencer is just as careful and deliberate with her language.

To further unpack Spencer's rhetorical public displays of privacy, I want to turn briefly to the opening lines of her poem "Any Wife to Any Husband." I will analyze this poem at length in chapter 2 and discuss how it reveals Spencer's environmental consciousness, but I offer this poem as a case study here because it occupied a privileged space in Spencer's consciousness in that it may be Spencer's most-revised poem. However, in spite of all the revisions she made, which included adding and deleting stanzas, changing the order of stanzas, and changing words, the opening line *never* changed.[15] This poem opens with seven poignant words that loudly declare a desire for privacy. The poem opens with the speaker saying, "This small garden is half my world." In the poem we are not told what the other half of her world is; this is left provocatively unclear. What appears to be a statement of transparency is, in fact, a denial of access into her private life. This statement actually says, "I am only telling you what half my world is; you will not know what the other half is." The speaker directs the reader's attention to a specific location: "this small garden." In doing so, the speaker sets the terms through which she is to be understood. We are to accept that the garden is "small" because she dictates that it is, and we must shift our attention to the garden and only the garden because this is the only part of her world to which we have access. In the opening line of the poem, this audacious speaker sets clear boundaries for her legibility and ensures that her privacy is intact. These opening lines symbolically function as a kind of velvet rope. The speaker is both audacious and duplicitous because she feigns transparency while simultaneously barring parts of herself from public access and legibility.

When Spencer wrote, she rarely followed prose logic, so her archive is filled with pages that contain words, sentences, thoughts that start from every angle of the page. In this way, her writing becomes more graphic and less script and produces a kind of visual eccentricity. What I am suggesting here is that it was not writing alone that sustained Spencer but also *how* she wrote that sustained her. Spencer quite literally wrote about whatever she chose and in the manner she chose. She made her own rules and established her own logics. In many cases, it is impossible to tell which orientation of the page is "correct" and where the writing begins and ends.

Her writing is legibly illegible. Experiencing the materiality of her archive and bearing witness to its idiosyncrasies helped me realize that *how* Spencer writes is indicative of how deliberately and carefully she controls her legibility. What I mean by this is that though order and logic in the traditional sense are not apparent to outsiders, Spencer was conscious of the archive she was constructing. Just as she knew where everything was on her staircase–filing cabinet, Spencer had an intimate knowledge of her archive. There is an intertextual element to her writings that illustrates that Spencer knew she was building *something*. Read in this context, the aforementioned "'leventy-leven bits" in so many different places also reflect Spencer's intimate knowledge of the contours of her archive as well as its possibilities that philosophically mirrors Amiri Baraka's poem "Black Art," in which he writes, "Let the world be a Black Poem" (Harris 220). Of course, Spencer's archive-building precedes Baraka's work, but what I am suggesting here is that Spencer was creating was a Black woman's world, and the intertextuality between her "bits" might reveal that she was constructing this Black world as a kind of Black poem, but this was a world and a poem legible and accessible only to Spencer. Though I was unable to decipher all of her handwriting, Spencer's archive does contain a poem manuscript that directly references Amiri Baraka (née LeRoi Jones) entitled "Leroi Meets Lincoln" or "When Abraham Lincoln Met Leroy Jones." Thus, my choice to invoke Baraka is intentional and alludes to a larger (perhaps indirect) argument I am making about Spencer, which is that, though her Blackness and politics were questioned, she saw herself in conversation with individuals who perhaps did not see themselves in conversation with her and certainly whom society did not see her in conversation with.

Recalling Spencer's staircase–filing cabinet, Spencer's guests probably would have (*mis*)interpreted her boxes as clutter, and even if they were able to review a piece of writing, they likely would have (*mis*)read it as incomplete, unfinished, and fragmentary. In the same way that Spencer's home archive is a material, physical experience, so is her institutional archive at the University of Virginia. Her papers and writings are "ordered" in a seemingly logical fashion with a detailed finding aid, but order, logic, and a finding aid were of little use to me when I engaged with her papers during the summer of 2016. The richness and beauty of her archive is that it will always be unknowable and mysterious. Her archive, like her writing, is legibly illegible.

Indeed, I suggest that Spencer's writing is just as careful and deliberate in such manuscripts as in those discussed above. Much like the "clutter" on her staircase, the graphic nature and visual eccentricity of her writing produces a kind of "clutter" that one can easily dismiss or mistake as drivel. What is curious about Spencer's writing is that she breaks the mandates of conventional prose logic *only* in these ephemeral writings, and her letters— those in her archive and the archives of her friends and colleagues—lack the visual eccentricity and graphic quality. The difference in these examples of Spencer's writing is evidence of a Spencer who censored herself when she was confronted with being published through normative channels that were not her own. However, I do not intend to suggest that Spencer loathed letter-writing as much as she disliked publication because, in reality, her archive is a testament to how much she enjoyed corresponding with friends and family. In many ways, her archive is also a testament to her appreciation for letters, more generally, because she carefully preserved the letters she received. Much to the chagrin of such individuals as Johnson, her writing in her letters was quite captivating and only increased his frustrations concerning her reluctance to publish: "Every time I get a good letter from you—and they are consistently good—I enjoy it so much it makes me mad. Mad because, despite the fact that you write finer, sharper, more brilliant prose than almost anybody I know, I cannot with all my entreating, cajoling or browbeating, get you to write the story that you could write so well" (qtd. in Greene 65). What I am suggesting here is that the measured, conventional prose by Spencer that we see in her personal correspondence is the same as the anthologized Spencer, the woman who was acutely aware of what she had to do to be legible in public spaces; this is a Spencer who is "playing by the rules," so to speak. Like the plants she carefully crossbred and planted in her garden, the graphic forms of her writing are a kind of plotting, planting, and cultivating that could exist in the Black woman's world she was building in her archive.

My attention to *how* Spencer wrote is one that is also concerned with how Spencer experienced the materiality of her writing. In other words, how did the writing process *feel* for her both emotionally and physically? The sensory nature of Spencer's archive is indeed a characteristic that makes it eccentric, but it is also a reflection of Spencer's physical writing experience. Writing was a very embodied experience for Spencer, one that caused her a significant amount of pain. She suffered from chronic arthritis in her hands most of her adult life, so writing was a very physically painful, labor-intensive task for her.[16] Ann Cvetkovich's assessment of the relationship between emotional and gay and lesbian archives provides insight into how we may understand Spencer's archive: "Understanding gay and lesbian archives as archives of emotion and trauma helps to explain some of their idiosyncrasies or, one might say, their 'queerness'" (242). I want to be careful here not to suggest that Spencer's archive or eccentricity are symptoms and manifestations of trauma. However, thinking of Spencer's archive as one that is imbued with her physical pain as well as her anxieties and meditations surrounding pub- licness and consumption certainly contextualizes both the visual and dis- cursive moments of eccentricity. Spencer inserted herself into her writings and her archive, and here I draw upon Brittney C. Cooper's term "embodied discourse" that is predicated on the belief that "we cannot divorce Black women's bodies from the theory they produce" (3).[17] Cooper uses this term in reference to Anna Julia Cooper's textual activism that she argues is also a hallmark of Black female textual activism:

> *Embodied discourse* refers to a form of Black female textual activism
> wherein race women assertively demand the inclusion of their bodies
> and, in particular, working-class Black bodies and Black female bodies
> by placing them in the texts they write and speak. By pointing to all
> the ways Black women's bodies emerge in formal and informal autobi-
> ographical accounts, archival materials, and advocacy work, we disrupt
> the smooth function of the culture of dissemblance and the politics
> of respectability as the paradigmatic frames through which to engage
> Black women's ideas and their politics. (3; emphasis original)

While it is not my intention to disrupt Spencer's attempts at secrecy or dissemblance, thinking about the materiality of her archive as embodied discourse is my way of honoring the way that she (and other Black women) produced knowledge and theorized and also of undermining aforemen- tioned critiques about Spencer's writing being "raceless" and "apolitical." Spencer does not appear to have kept a diary in the traditional sense, but her writings function as a cataloging of her thoughts. In reference to poetry, she writes, "they are *me* in the years here [;] they are my conversation with myself" (emphasis added).[18] In other words, Spencer's archive is a sen- sory experience because it is not simply an archive of writings; it is also an archive of her emotions about writing and an archive of the materials she laid her hands upon and transformed into her canvases for her writings. And if her poetry was the "me in the years here," her archive is also a repre- sentation of her being.

An analysis of Spencer's eccentricity would not be complete without examining her gender performance and views of motherhood. As noted in the introduction, this work is not a biographical endeavor, but I want to discuss some biographical elements of Spencer's life to gain insight into how she fostered the "creative sparks" within her life that enabled her to carefully construct such a unique archive and pen thousands of poems during the Nadir in the South while married and raising three children. Spencer's liberatory vision of Black womanhood extended to motherhood as well, and her writings reveal that she viewed mothering and motherhood as practices that extended beyond the biological realm. Spencer anticipates the writings of female Black Arts Movement poets such as Sonia Sanchez and Audre Lorde who advanced the idea of "radical mothering" in which notions of traditional motherhood were expansive and applied to more than just the rearing of one's biological child. This notion of "radical mothering" also referred to nurturing one's self, one's community, or one's fellow Black sister.[19] Thus, by invoking this tradition of gardening, Spencer offers a vision of "expansive mothering," in which "motherhood" and "mothering" are not exclusively biological acts, and she is able to advance the notions of Black womanhood that both are diverse and encourage individual empowerment. I want to be careful here and note that I am not arguing that Spencer was doing the same kind of work as the Black Arts Movement poets, who were more explicit with their appropriation of mothering. Rather, I am interested in how Spencer created a mothering ethos for herself and how the fashioning of this ethos is an example of her eccentricity.

Spencer was an untypical woman who enjoyed an unusual amount of leisure, especially for a southern Black woman in the Jim Crow era. Her ability to enjoy such leisure and autonomy was due to Edward Spencer's resourcefulness and desire for Anne and his family to live a life of comfort.[20] She married Edward in 1901, moved into the 1313 Pierce Street home in Lynchburg in 1903, and by 1906 she had the couple's three children (Greene 44). I aim to be careful in my use of "leisure," as not to suggest that Anne Spencer enjoyed a life of luxury. She was still a southern, Black woman at the mercy of Jane Crow. Though "class" is a very complicated, often unreliable descriptor with regard to Black families, I would characterize the Spencer family as "deceptively Black middle class." Anne's "unusual" amount of leisure, a term Greene also uses, is due to Edward's work ethic and unrivaled business savvy and tenacity (46). Edward's primary employment was at the United States Post Office as a mail carrier, and he made history as Lynchburg's first Black mail carrier. He also owned a grocery/hardware store with his brother, and he invested in real estate (Greene 44). He single-handedly made additions and improvements to the family home (Greene 44–45). The archival materials suggest that Edward had multiple businesses. Accounting ledgers show that he had some sort of chicken business, though it is unclear exactly what it was. He also held a chauffeur's license and had a chauffeur business. Edward's workload meant that he slept only a few hours per night, but his labor was truly performed with love and a desire to allow Anne to focus on her writing.

Spencer briefly taught at her alma mater, Virginia Theological Seminary and College, from 1912 to 1914, but she remained unemployed by choice until she became a librarian at Dunbar High School in 1924. She remained in this position until 1946. Before becoming a librarian, Spencer occupied her time as she desired, and she was able to spend her days free from pressing obligations:

> So before she went to Dunbar High School as librarian, Annie Spencer had what her son [Chauncey Spencer] described as an easy life. Her routine would be to sleep until eleven, bathe until noon, and sit before the window and brush her hair until about two, when she would dress and come downstairs about three in the afternoon. She would spend the rest of the day in her garden working with the plants or in the garden house writing and reading. Sometimes she would join the family for dinner, but more often (especially after she went to work) she would take her dinner tray to the garden house and remain there until dark. In the evenings she would spend time with the family. But when the entire household was asleep, she could be found reading and writing until two or three in the morning. (Greene 47)

I offer the above biographical anecdotes to illustrate that just as Spencer performed her womanhood on her own terms, she performed womanhood and motherhood on her own terms, and her performance was very careful. While one can simply focus on the aforementioned idiosyncrasies and stop there, asking *why* Spencer adopted such a routine and *what* it symbolized for her is crucial. Spencer *deliberately* delegated the day-to-day tasks of motherhood and adopted a routine that was rooted in self-care and self-cultivation. Even while she worked as a librarian, the basis of the routine remained unchanged. The approaches she utilized in gardening—innovation and creativity—she carried into motherhood, and she mothered herself.

In the above passage, Spencer's son describes his mother's daily schedule as "easy." On the surface, these rituals of hair brushing for hours and extensive moments of solitude may seem selfish or suggest a lack of interest in motherhood entirely. Rather, Spencer's daily rituals illustrate that she had a reimagined view of mothering, one that prioritized her own well-being. Spencer's daily practice is a profound example of the ways in which she negotiated a space to exist. By modeling and adopting a daily practice of self-care, Spencer stands in opposition to McDougald's belief that New Negro women must settle for a life of self-abnegation. In "Any Wife to Any Husband," Spencer writes, "This small garden is half my world," and her son's insight into her routine illustrates how she *lived* this mantra daily (Greene 186). In this way, Spencer anticipates the work of such Black feminist writers as Audre Lorde, who in 1988 wrote, "Caring for myself is not self-indulgence, it is self-preservation, and that is an act of political warfare" (*Burst* 131). For a Black woman to perform such deliberate acts of self-care is both subversive and radical, especially in the Jim Crow South. Through each brushstroke of her hair and hour spent asleep, Spencer undermines dominant narratives about Black womanhood and redefines it on her own terms. And once again, I want to invoke gardening as the work of a gardener. Thinking about gardening in this way allows me to position Spencer as both an artist and the product of her own artwork because, indeed, there is a skillful imagination to her daily routine.

Notice that her son recalls his mother retiring to her garden and writing until the early hours of the morning with hours dedicated to tending to her garden. What Chauncey describes as an "easy" schedule is the work of deliberate and daring cultivation. Spencer's routine embodies an intimate self-connection and self-awareness that embodies Audre Lorde's theory of the erotic: "For once we begin to feel deeply all the aspects of our lives, we begin to demand from ourselves and from our life-pursuits that they feel in accordance with that joy which we know ourselves to be capable of" (*Sister Outsider* 57). The small garden Spencer speaks of in "Any Wife to Any Husband" did not become "half her world" by sheer happenstance. Spencer had to do the work to make it a reality; she had to discover and cultivate her erotic knowledge. Indeed, Edward's economic support allowed her time, but she had to perform the work of cultivation, and she did so courageously.

In reality, motherhood figured very strongly into Spencer's life and thinking, and her archive is filled with her children's and grandchildren's drawings, homework assignments, notes, and familial ephemera. Spencer, however, did not allow the obligations of matrimony and motherhood to constrain her. Frischkorn and Rainey explain that "although she enjoyed the creative outlets of domesticity and child rearing, she delegated many of those duties to housekeepers so she could focus her energies on her poetry and her garden, as well as her involvement in civil rights issues" (15). Spencer did not keep everything; she kept the things that were important and had meaning to her. While she wrote poems about her marriage and, specifically about her husband, Edward, Spencer's published poetry does not reflect motherhood. That Spencer's intimate thoughts on motherhood and parenting were left out of the public sphere is another example of her public display of privacy, and we can recall that although the speaker of her poem names "this small garden" as "half her world," the other half of her world is unnamed, and neither marriage nor children figure into the poem. An unpublished, undated poem entitled "Amends" expresses a maternalism that is usually not found in her poetry:

There never was another morn so dark
As that dark morn.
The early day's work belched
Up to a leaden sky
My eyes mirrored the ugly night faces
Of men moved by habit and
Were still asleep
Their eyes heed my own thankless fare:
Because I who could sing should
Lack the time for song.
Cold black early morning
Is day's part to commit murder
But there are brighter suns
Than the sun:
My iced fingers seeking their next
In my coat found the warm suede glove dropped from my baby's hand—
There never was [an]other morn so
Bright as that bright morn![21]

I want to juxtapose the title of poem with the line in which the speaker names her baby's glove. The word "Amends" has multiple meanings that signal improvement, compensation, and a move toward "rightness." After the speaker invokes her baby, there is an abrupt, brief shift in the tone of the poem, and it moves from being the darkest day of the speaker's life to the brightest day. A transformation takes place both within the speaker and within the poem, but the speaker's transformation is marked only by an elusive em dash. While it is a reasonable to conclude that this move toward improvement is due to the speaker's memory of her baby, the speaker offers no additional information, as if to say that her experience as a mother and meditations on motherhood are not for public consumption. This is the only poem in her archive that I found that explicitly concerned motherhood, and I do not think it unusual at all that it contains a speaker much like the speaker in "Any Wife to Any Husband" who reveals virtually nothing about her private life. Here, the em dash functions as a literal velvet rope that, once again, denies the reader access into her private life and private thoughts. Once again, what appears to be a statement of transparency is an insistence upon privacy. "Amends" is indeed a poem that reflects Spencer's meditations on motherhood, and her thoughts on motherhood were that they needed to remain private. In chapter 3, I discuss an undated, unpublished manuscript entitled "Love and Gardens" in which Spencer does theorize a relationship between gardening, God, and parenting, but, as I note there, the document reveals more about her relationship to God and the natural world than about her own personal views on motherhood. Spencer was very private about her personal life even though she was an avid entertainer and host. Spencer had a son who died shortly after his birth (Greene 44). The loss of her child is not the subject of her published poems, and the materials available in her archive do not explicitly mention this profound loss. "Amends" illustrates that though Spencer may not have outwardly performed motherhood in ways that were both normative and legible to those around her, it was a central part of her identity, and, like her writing, it was something that she protected and cultivated. It was the work of a gardener.

When I originally embarked on this archival project, I intended to write a cultural history of her literary salon during the New Negro Renaissance, and, at first, I was both frustrated and disappointed that the documents that I was hoping to find were not present. It was not what I expected. And this is what I have come to admire and respect about Anne Spencer: that she is boldly odd and unusual in ways that I would not have expected and in ways not traditionally associated with Blackness and Black womanhood. Writing is an act of self-representation, and Spencer's careful, albeit, unusual writing practice represented that, like her garden, she did not exist for others' consumption.

The stunning contribution Spencer makes through her archive is that it makes us think about what poetry is, where it is found, and how it is created. This also serves as a reminder of what Alice Walker tells us in *In Search of Our Mothers' Gardens* when she writes about the "creative spark" and inherent artistry with which Black women live their lives (240).

Though I indeed have analyzed her poetry, I also want to suggest that everything I have presented here is her poetry and is intended to highlight the poetry Spencer created in her daily life. Spencer's garden is her poetry; her rising at eleven in the morning and brushing her hair for two hours is her poetry; and her "'leventy-leven bits" and boxes on her staircase are her poetry. Because Spencer wrote on everything, everything becomes her poetry. Spencer's eccentricity is her poetry.

2

"This Small Garden Is Half My World"

Anne Spencer's Ecopoetics

What is gained when Spencer's garden and her poetics are juxtaposed is an invitation to position nature as a site of Black feminist epistemology. Spencer offers another way of thinking about *being,* namely how Black women articulate their womanhood and their humanness. This chapter honors the natural world as a legitimate site of Black feminist epistemology and analyzes the ways Spencer uses the natural world to articulate her *beingness.* Bringing together her garden, poetics, and her feminist inclinations, this chapter is ultimately an analysis of Spencer's gender politics and her meditations on Black womanhood. It seeks to understand how she articulates these meditations using the language and symbolism of the natural world. Using ecopoetics as an analytical framework enables questions to shift from, *Why a garden?* to *What is revealed when Spencer mediates her beingness through her garden, and what are the implications for Black womanhood?* This chapter locates Spencer within a tradition of Black feminist thought and demonstrates that Spencer's poetry is inextricably linked to her lived experience as a Black woman. Thus, her poetics and discursive strategies implicate all Black women. Many of Spencer's poems are infused with natural world imagery; however, for the purpose of this examination, the poems "[Earth, I thank you]," "Any Wife to Any Husband," and "He Said:" are considered, as both the natural world and notions of Black womanhood are the central themes. In these "nature poems," Spencer articulates a profound sense of desire for and connectedness to the natural world, and it becomes particularly clear that for Spencer her garden was not only a source of inspiration; it was an extension of herself. Spencer's unpublished, undated prose piece "Love and Gardens" is also utilized, as it provides rare insight into her thoughts on motherhood.

A carefully chosen collection of fruit trees, herbs, and flowers, some of which she crossbred herself, Anne Spencer's garden was a testament to her improvisational energy and creative flair. Spencer's garden was a profoundly generative, sustaining space for her both creatively and existentially. As Rebecca T. Frischkorn and Reuben M. Rainey explain, her garden, much like her writing, provided a space of infinite possibilities and was to be enjoyed simply as a space of pleasure she created: "Anne's garden reveals the vitality and bold experimentation of the self-taught designer that she was. . . . Anne's garden was clearly a horticultural endeavor, not an agricultural one, and it was planted for beauty, not for harvest. Anne Spencer created her garden as an ideal world unto itself, a sanctuary to nurture and sustain herself, her family, her neighbors, and her friends" (29, 47). Frischkorn and Rainey are careful to note that Spencer's garden was not for consumption; it was simply to be appreciated autonomously. Spencer's reluctance to publish her writing echoes her aversion toward objectification, containment, commodification (and career and literary posterity in the usual sense). The desire to simply exist freely and unencumbered is also how she envisioned Black womanhood. Her garden indeed served as a site of self-fashioned, self-defined pleasure and artistic inspiration, but, more importantly, her garden figured her Black womanhood. Her garden, a symbol of staunch individuality and innovation, mirrored the type of Black womanhood she performed daily and represented a vision she held for all Black women.

What becomes evident when we examine Spencer's poetry is that she is acutely aware of the importance of self-fashioned pleasure in her life as a Black woman, and by inserting her garden in her poetry, Spencer arguably makes the claim that this type of self-fashioned pleasure should be enjoyed by all Black women. Thus, what emerges is a Black feminist rhetoric, and we see that Spencer is not only concerned with Black women's survival; she also is concerned with their happiness, and she claims that it is their right. Thus, what we see in Spencer's poems is both an articulation of a Black environmental imaginary and the emergence of a New Negro woman rhetoric in which the New Negro woman is an *individual* whose body and destiny can be defined, negotiated, and created on her own terms. Though these two themes of a Black environmental imaginary and Black womanhood may appear contradictory or unrelated, Spencer's poetry demonstrates that the two are not only complementary but inextricably linked, and Spencer's life is a testament to the fact that her sense of her own womanhood was predicated on her ability to connect with the natural world and cultivate her own garden. When juxtaposed, what emerges is a representation of individual Black womanhood and a politics of self-care; Spencer illustrates that the nurturing and cultivating of her garden is an act of self-nurturing and self-cultivation. In doing so, Spencer anticipates the writings of Black Arts Movement and Black feminist writers such as Sonia Sanchez, Audre Lorde, and Ntozake Shange in advancing a rhetoric of self-care, and through her ecopoetics, she creates openings through which subsequent Black female poets can reimagine and re-create both the natural world and Black womanhood.[1]

By writing about her own intimate relationship with the natural world, Spencer effectively accomplishes two feats. First, she allows the reader to experience the natural world from an African American individual's perspective, a perspective that has been both historically silenced and negated. Second, she provides a representation of a Black female body asserting her own subjectivity and engaged in an act of pleasure. Thus, Spencer's poetry can be seen as corrective and revisionist in that it challenges dominant narratives about both Black engagement with the natural world and Black womanhood. Through her writing, Spencer reclaims the natural world and recasts it as a space that African American individuals have a right to experience intimately. That Spencer uses the natural world to challenge these tropes is significant because garden imagery symbolizes rebirth and within the context of her poems, what is being birthed are new narratives about both African Americans' environmental consciousness and Black womanhood.

Western understandings of humans' relationship to the environment posit that human beings are dominant over the natural world and nonhuman creatures. This thinking stems, in part, from the Hebrew Bible in Genesis 1:28, which reads: "And God blessed them, and God said unto them, 'Be fruitful and multiply, and replenish the earth, and subdue it; and have dominion over the fish of the sea, and over the fowl of the air, and over every living thing that moveth upon the earth'" (KJ21). This notion of dominion, however, did not extend to Black individuals. As Carolyn Finney explains in *Black Faces, White Spaces,* ideologies about African Americans and their relationship to the environment were being developed at the same time as other racial ideologies, and Black people have been systematically and institutionally denied access to the environment just as they have been excluded and alienated from other facets of American society (35). Both in American society and in the American literary imagination, the outdoors is represented as a "white space"; however, Blacks are deeply, intimately, and historically connected to the environment, and their stories have yet to be told; their environmental imaginaries have yet to be considered. This deep, intimate, spiritual connection to the natural world is clearly seen in the poetry of Anne Spencer, as it was her renowned garden at her home in Lynchburg, Virginia, that served as her muse. Both Spencer's daily life and poetry were "interwoven with her garden," and through her poetry, we see the significance of the natural world from the often-negated perspective of an African American individual (Frischkorn and Rainey 45). In addition to providing a voice for Black environmental imaginaries, Spencer's poetry also challenges pervasive stereotypes specific to Black women and their bodies.

In *Laboring Women,* Jennifer L. Morgan explains that African women and their bodies were fraught with oppressive myths and stereotypes inscribed during slavery, ones that rendered them grotesque vessels of biological and economic reproduction (7, 16, 28). Furthermore, the types of labor women performed during slavery coupled with racist projected sexual anxieties cast Black women as "the long-suffering and desexualized Mammy, the primitive Topsy, the exotic Jezebel, and the evil, emasculating Sapphire" (qtd. in Wallace-Sanders 3). Such mythoi and notions specifically pathologized Black female bodies and were what Black female writers were forced to contend with both individually and creatively as they attempted to create literary representations of African American women (Wallace-Sanders 3). As a Black woman writing about nature in an intimate fashion and looking to nature for inspiration, Spencer undermines these tropes because she illustrates that her Black body and the natural world are not inharmonious; rather, through her poetry, she suggests that they share a symbiotic relationship. This suggestion is further underscored by the reality that Spencer found immense joy and solace within her own garden. Just as the various elements of her garden were not to be consumed, Black womanhood is not to be co-opted or corrupted. What is unique and remarkable about Spencer's poetry is that she offers a vision of Black womanhood and the natural world that exists beyond the ideologies of dominion; she offers an alternative way of being and thinking about being.

Though Spencer's poetry has received minimal scholarly attention and critical engagement, she both wrote and published during the New Negro Movement. Her discursive strategies and representations of the Black female body parallel those of the more "canonical" New Negro women writers, such as Nella Larsen and Jessie Fauset, who advocated for the New Negro woman's right to happiness, self-determinism, and pleasure and penned novels featuring self-determined Black female protagonists. When situated within the context of the New Negro Renaissance, Spencer's poetry is highly subversive (and arguably even more overtly subversive than the work of her more critically acclaimed contemporaries). Spencer's nature poems serve as a counternarrative to the natural world as a "white space," and, by placing her Black female body and her garden within her poetry, she offers a representation of Black femininity and womanhood that also challenges dominant tropes about Black women's bodies. J. Lee Greene explains that though Spencer's poetry is not overtly "racially oriented," she was deeply concerned with "the race question," and I elaborate on Greene's conclusions by illustrating that Spencer was both racially oriented and especially concerned with the plight of Black women and their right to joy and happiness (128). That Spencer celebrates her garden in poetic form is not only indicative of how essential the natural world is to her creativity as an artist; it also, as mentioned above, illustrates that her garden served an existential purpose within her life as a Black woman because it was both something that she *created* and a space to which she assigned meaning and from which she received pleasure.

Dianne D. Glave explains that part of the reason that African Americans' relationship to the natural world has been negated is that, particularly during enslavement, environmentalism was communicated in forms that were not understood by whites, as it was both personal and beyond ideologies of colonization and dominion, and therefore denied: "African Americans characterized the soil or land in their own way. Though they cultivated Southern land, they did not express a sense of entitlement or ownership over it, nor did they generally subscribe to the white notion of land 'belonging' to people.... Such forms of identification and connectedness with the environment have been largely ignored by whites because they do not fit the white paradigm of land ownership or even their conceptualization of wilderness" (*Rooted in the Earth* 8, 9). Thus, part of what Spencer is doing in her poetry is providing evidence of an existing Black environmental consciousness, and her poetry provides both an aperture through which we may see and analyze Black individuals' relationship to the environment and challenges dominant narratives that posit the natural world as a "white space." This insight is articulated through a Black feminist lens, as Spencer's ecological consciousness is inextricably linked to her lived experience as a Black woman. It is not my intention to identify Spencer as a Black feminist. Though such language may have been available to her, her archive, as discussed in chapter 1, suggests a disdain for categorization and labeling. Rather, I want to illustrate how her poetic choices reveal an attention to "the Negro question" and "the woman question" and therefore align with Black feminist thought.

Spencer's critical environmental consciousness is present and clearly articulated in her untitled poem ["Earth, I thank you"], in which she expresses an intimate sense of connectedness to and gratitude for the inspiration the natural world provides:

Earth, I thank you
for the pleasure of your language
You've had a hard time
bringing it to me
from the ground
to grunt thru the noun
To all the way
Feeling   seeing   smelling   touching
—awareness
I am here! (Greene 197)

In this sensual poem, Spencer establishes the natural world as her muse, and by thanking the earth for the pleasure of its language, Spencer underscores that her appreciation goes beyond a superficial admiration of its aesthetic qualities. By stating she finds pleasure in the language of the natural world, Spencer makes the claim that she both communicates with and understands the natural world. This statement is a powerful claim because it not only suggests that she, as a Black woman, possesses an environmental consciousness that should be accounted for, but it also underscores as a myth the ubiquitous notion that Blacks are inherently alienated from nature and deeply unattached to the natural world. Spencer continues to refute the myth of deep detachment in the latter portion of the poem, as the words "feeling, seeing, smelling, touching" denote not just a connectedness to the natural world but also a sense of unity and harmony. This is not a relationship predicated on hierarchy and dominion. In the final line, Spencer signals to the reader that she has a symbiotic relationship with the natural world.

The final words, "I am here!," are a bold declaration, and in this moment Spencer is speaking both as a poet and a Black woman. As a poet, this statement emphasizes that the natural world is her muse. The "pleasure" of its "language" inspires her work and creates an "awareness" that grants her both the ability and subject matter to write; therefore, this statement is a humble act of obeisance from Spencer and an acknowledgment that her art and status as a poet would not be possible without the natural world. If we consider the magnitude of this statement from Spencer's perspective as a Black woman, this statement carries a profound existential meaning because Spencer is thanking the natural world for its ability to provide her with "pleasure," which translates to happiness. In other words, Spencer is showing gratitude that the natural world allows her, as a Black woman, to be fulfilled, whole, and *human*. Thus, as the poem progresses, Spencer transitions from expressing gratitude to the natural world as a source of creativity to articulating a sense of indebtedness to the natural world for making her existence, as a Black female poet, both possible and meaningful. In this sense, the poem culminates in an image of birth, as Spencer implicitly names the earth as her mother.

Notice that the speaker acknowledges that the earth had "a hard time" bringing its language to her. This reference can certainly signal the fraught history between Blacks and the natural world, underscoring that the color line extends to the natural world. "Hard time" also signals that there is a generative theme in this poem, so there is a sense that the earth is giving birth to something. The "hard time" referenced in the third line juxtaposed with the "grunt" in the sixth line evokes physical contractions of childbirth, so the earth is positioned as a laboring mother giving birth to Spencer, the Black woman-poet-human, whose birth is honored and confirmed with the exclamatory sentence, "I am here!" This generative theme is also cyclical because the earth gives birth to Spencer, who in turn gives birth to her poetry. The phrase "grunt thru the noun" also evokes the creative process of writing and the difficulties of writer's block, so there are two types of labor and birthing present in this poem. That Spencer invokes such a vivid, material experience underscores how she views her materiality through the lens of the natural world. For Black women, in particular, the ecofeminist critique against the conflation of "woman" and "nature" is especially germane because colonialism rendered Black women's bodies as kind of natural resource that was both perpetually available and exploitable. As Paul Outka explains, Black people were associated with nature to the extent that, like nature, they were to be domesticated: "It was not simply the treatment of black people as if they were a part of nature that underpinned slavery, in other words, but in making black people coextensive with a nature that existed solely to be exploited and 'improved' by whites" (53). Spencer's use of "I am here" departs from this pejorative association, instead positioning nature as a generative space.

Notice that the poem shifts from the speaker addressing the earth to the speaker making a declaration. The words "I am here" symbolize the birth of an autonomous subject. It is a powerful moment of self-recognition in which the speaker names and identifies herself as a subject. The dash that precedes "I am here" suggests that the speaker is having an existential moment in real time, and we witness the speaker transcend and come to the realization that who she is as a poet and human being is because of the natural world. The ability to name one's subjectivity and hereness reflects a profound sense of rootedness and groundedness, and this comes from the speaker's intimate identification with the natural world. Like the natural world, ideologies about Black womanhood and Black women's bodies have historically existed as constructions that serve the purposes, fantasies, and desires of others. The speaker's naming herself signals a refusal to have her personhood co-opted, and that she alone will define herself. The words "I am here" are punctuated with an exclamation mark, making this existential moment double as a proclamation. The speaker is shouting, forcing the reader to listen and implicitly demanding that we respect her sovereignty. Similar to Celie's statement in Alice Walker's *The Color Purple*, "I'm pore, I'm black, I may be ugly and can't cook, . . . But I'm here" (207), this is a transformative moment of self-recognition, and, in particular, the recognition of Black womanhood.

This idea of the natural world as having both creative and existential meaning for Spencer is prevalent throughout her work. Through her use of the natural world, Spencer is able to disrupt prevalent myths about both Black environmental consciousness and Black womanhood. The poem "Any Wife to Any Husband" is emblematic of the way Spencer infuses her critical environmental consciousness with notions of Black womanhood. The poem opens with seven compelling words: "This small garden is half my world" (Greene 186). The statement "This small garden is half my world" is both profound and radical because in saying that this small garden is "half [her] world," Spencer is making the powerful claim that she, as a Black woman, has the right to shape and define her experience in the world. In doing so, she is boldly asserting her subjectivity and articulating that she is not a mere passive recipient who will have the world thrust upon her; rather, she will make meaning of the world in the manner that resonates with her experience. It is important to note that Spencer does not state what the other half of her world is; this is left provocatively unclear. However, that she names the garden illustrates and underscores the importance and the privileged space it occupies within her life and private thoughts. In other words, the significance of her garden supersedes her roles as both mother and wife, which are social obligations and expectations, and she offers a possibility of womanhood in which one's priorities can exist outside of the limitations of traditional notions of "a woman's sphere."[2]

Spencer's garden is a space that she both *chose* and *created*. She names her garden as such, decides its location, its dimension, and its composition; she calls it into being, so her role as gardener also assumes a divine quality. Spencer refers to her garden as "small," which is a highly relative, subjective term. However, even its current restored condition, the garden measures 40 feet wide and 195 feet in length with garden pools and Anne's writing cottage, Edankraal (Frischkorn and Rainey 27). Objectively speaking, it is hardly "small." But it is small because Spencer says it is, so through this statement, Spencer is not just creating space; she is also redefining it. Thus, in addition to the garden existing beyond the purview of the domestic sphere, it exists beyond the possible corruption and authority of anyone other than herself; it is a protected, autonomous space that is subject only to her imagination. Keeping in mind the kind of space the garden is for Spencer, namely that it is a space of joy, what this statement also reveals is that Spencer is clearly stating the importance of her happiness and well-being; the opening line of her poem could be rewritten as: "Happiness is half my world." What we see here just in the opening line is that Spencer is offering a vision of Black womanhood in which agency, self-fashioning, and personal satisfaction are central.

We see Spencer's discursive strategies employed through her use of the title "Any Wife to Any Husband," which originates from a Robert Browning poem with the same title. Though Spencer borrows Browning's title, the intent of her poem is drastically different and destabilizes traditional notions of womanhood. Spencer invokes the traditional notion of femininity of Browning's poem only to subvert it, erecting a new vision of Black womanhood in its place. In Browning's poem, the female speaker expresses matrimonial affection for her husband and articulates his centrality in her life; Spencer's poem expresses her love for her *garden,* a space she created, and neither a husband nor matrimony figures into her thinking or appears in the poem. What Spencer does here is radically rewrite Browning's poem from an *independent* Black woman's perspective. Poet and critic Holly Karapetkova contends that such discursive strategies illustrate that Spencer's artistic choices were "profoundly modern, black, and female" (229): "Far from merely mimicking writers like Browning and Yeats, Spencer takes their tradition (and the art long held to be the province solely of white men) and uses it to protest the exclusion and neglect of voices like her own. The fact that we are still able to hear her voice clearly through her poems—the voice of a black woman continually questioning the exclusive whiteness and maleness that dominated modernist writing—marks the triumph of her art" (Karapetkova 240).

That Spencer invokes a Victorian poet and Victorian ideals of womanhood is also of importance because, as noted above, the ideologies surrounding true womanhood were reserved exclusively for white female bodies. By rewriting the poem, Spencer symbolically writes Black women's bodies into an ideology of womanhood and suggests that Black women and their bodies are capable of womanhood. However, Spencer is not championing the nineteenth-century "true womanhood" ideology that espoused a singular vision of womanhood and equated (white) "femininity" with "the domestic sphere." Neither is she espousing reductive notions of "the domestic sphere" or suggesting that such a thing as "a woman's place" exists. Rather, Spencer offers an alternative vision of Black womanhood, one that can be both expressed and fashioned individually; for Spencer, it is a womanhood in which the natural world and the happiness that it brings to her life are central and "half her world." Thus, what appears on the surface to be an homage to a Browning poem becomes a site of contestation through which reductive, exclusionary notions of white womanhood are challenged and a new, inclusive notion of Black womanhood is established. Spencer's use of Browning's title is also a discursive strategy in that, by changing the content of the poem, the title thus transforms into a double entendre as well. Though it does invoke Browning's original poem, it can be read as an instructional poem for Black women. In other words, the lines of this poem are "for to any Black wife to say her husband." Read as an instructional poem, the statement, "This small garden is half my world," becomes a kind of call to action for Black women to both demand and assert their right to define the world on their own terms. Spencer symbolically models the new Black womanhood with this powerful claim, and, in doing so, implicitly asks Black women, "What is half your world?" and encourages them to define it. Spencer's implicit question envisions a woman's "place" as an entity of her own fashioning and creation and should be a generative, liberatory space.

In saying that the garden is half her world, Spencer also articulates her relationship to the natural world, and this statement is a form of environmental claims-making in that Spencer states that she, as a Black woman, has both the *innate* ability and the right to experience a deep sense of connectedness to the natural world. In the same way that this statement can be interpreted as a new Black womanhood for all Black women, this statement can also be interpreted as a form of environmental claims-making that implicates all African American individuals. Implicit in Spencer's statement is not only an invitation for Black women to define their worlds but by modeling the connectedness with the natural world, she demonstrates that the level of intimacy she has is a possibility for other African American individuals, not just Black women. In other words, what Spencer is also saying is, "This garden is half *our* world." Through this symbolic claims-making, Spencer challenges the pervasive myth that African Americans lack environmental consciousness, and in the subsequent eight lines of the poem, Spencer stresses the importance of the legacy that her garden leaves behind:

> I am nothing to it—when all is said,
> I plant the thorn and kiss the rose,
> But they will grow when I am dead.
>
> Let not this change, Love, the human life
> Share with her the joy you had with me,
> List her with the plaintive bird you heard with me,
> Feel all human joys, but
> Feel most a "shadowy third." (Greene 186)

Spencer minimizes the role she plays in cultivating her garden to emphasize that while she is a mortal creature, the natural world, as symbolized through her garden, is eternal. The way Spencer's garden is depicted in his poem is illustrative of how garden imagery is utilized in many of her poems in that it is used to represent "ideals, such as love, beauty, and immortality" (Greene 109).

Though the opening line of the poem initially gives the impression that Spencer will be expressing why the poem is half her world, in this latter portion of the poem, Spencer transitions from talking about the poem's importance to her and shifts to discussing the garden's significance to others. In saying that "they [the roses] will grow when I am dead" and encouraging her garden to "share with her the joy you had with me," Spencer extends an invitation to others to enjoy the connectedness and intimacy with the natural world that she has. The "her" Spencer references is ambiguous and could refer to "Love." Frischkorn and Rainey suggest that the "her" in the poem refers to another woman and argue that "the poet employs a metaphor of the garden and specifically the relationship between the garden and the gardener as a means of speculating about a possible future connection with a husband after the death of his wife" (63). However, what is clear is that the speaker does not want the practice of gardening to cease after her death. More importantly, she does not want the *joy* of gardening to cease. Notice in the sixth line she shifts to addressing her garden and delivers an imperative that continues on to the seventh line, "Share with her the joy you had with me/List with her the plaintive bird you heard with me" (Greene 186). In other words, the poet's request is simply this: "Please take care of one another." In the same way that her opening statement, "This small garden is half my world," implicitly addresses and implicates Black women, this "her" could be not only an implicit invitation for Black women to find joy in the natural world; it also can be read as both an urgent plea and invitation to Black women to continue the practice of gardening. In this moment, Spencer is invoking the cultural legacy of gardening within the African American tradition and its particular significance to African American women. In doing so, Spencer calls the reader's attention to the fact that this legacy exists and therefore an African American environmental imaginary exists, and this latter portion of the poem can be interpreted as an urgent plea to Black women to continue the tradition of gardening, which is also a metaphor for self-cultivation. As a self-taught horticulturist, Spencer certainly would have wanted Black women to continue the tradition of gardening. Equally important, though, is that women create and cultivate their own spaces of happiness.

The practice of gardening has a long-standing tradition in African American history, one that is of particular significance for African American women. During enslavement, African American women cultivated gardens for reasons that were both economic and personal: "Gardens served as sources of food for women's families, means of enhancing their homes, and, in some circumstances, small sources of revenue. The women improved their families' nutrition with homegrown vegetables and saved money by limiting the use of store-bought goods. . . . The women also created visual appeal in the feminine domain with flowers and ornamental plants outside their homes" (Glave, *Rooted in the Earth* 121–22). These gardens were also powerful tools of agency and resistance for Black womanhood, as African American women could autonomously assert and perform their femininity in these spaces. As previously noted, Black women and their bodies were inscribed with subjugative meaning through slavery and were consequently excluded from the possibility of aspiring to the "cult of domesticity and true womanhood"; this cult of a "new Eve" was reserved exclusively for white women. Thus, in many ways, Black women's gardens were a means through which they could stake a claim in the domestic sphere as well as a vehicle for Black aesthetic and spiritual expression.

I want to highlight a few elements of Spencer's garden because it was—and still is—a glorious work of art. For Spencer, her place of refuge was her garden because, like writing poetry, gardening was a space for artistic ingenuity, one in which she could cultivate and refine her craft. When we read Spencer's poetry alongside her garden, we see the full scope—and brilliance—of her artistry. For this reason, I read Spencer's garden as a kind of supplemental, alternative archive that complements the collection at the University of Virginia. As Rebecca T. Frischkorn and Reuben M. Rainey note, Spencer's garden is quite similar to her poetry in the sense it was it was a work of art that was constantly in revision: "She reworked her garden in a similar manner [to her poems]—enlarging, re-crafting, and refining it over a period of seventy years" (27). And just as with her poetry, she playfully invokes tradition only to subvert it. In the same way that "Any Wife to Any Husband" appears to mimic Browning, her garden, at first glance, looks like a traditional Virginia residential garden. It has four carefully crafted, distinct "rooms," and such elements as Virginia red cedars make this garden appear like a replica of some of the popular small residential gardens of her day.[3] These ornamental small residential gardens carry the same racialized, classed, and gendered connotations of true womanhood ideology because they were symbols and extensions of white femininity and a dominion-oriented ethos that positions the natural world as an object to be tamed. In spite of the visual similarity, Spencer's garden deviated from a traditional Virginia residential garden in distinctive ways, ones that are evocative of her poetry. In the same way Spencer makes room for her Black female voice in her writing, she infused her garden with her personal flair, a flair that is reminiscent of African American vernacular gardens. Such elements as bold experimentation with color, use of recycled materials, and her transplanting flowers and shrubs from the wild are more in line with African American vernacular gardens. In true vernacular garden tradition, Spencer resourcefully—and imaginatively—used the materials that were available to her with the most essential arguably being her imagination and vision (Frischkorn and Rainey 30). Her garden had a fragmentary composition, and, here, one cannot help but be reminded of her striking use of ephemera—the "'leventy-leven bits"—for her poems.

Spencer's harmonious relationship with the natural world cannot be overstated so while her garden may not have been for others' consumption, it also was not simply ornamental or decorative though it was beautiful. Perhaps one of the most important ways Spencer's garden deviates from a traditional garden and embodies the spirit of a vernacular garden is that she shared her garden with her friends and family. Her children played there, and family weddings and celebrations were held there. It was communal space, one that offered sanctuary for loved ones, her local Lynchburg community, and guests. Thank-you notes from friends express gratitude not just for her hospitality but also admiration for her garden, indicating that, like Georgia Douglas Johnson, they did not separate Spencer from her garden. But her garden was an invitation to separate the natural world from trauma, a task that could be daunting for Black people. In his 1947 essay "My Adventures as a Social Poet," Langston Hughes articulates the heft of the fear of the natural world:

> Poets who write mostly about love, roses, and moonlight, sunsets and snow, must lead a very quiet life. Seldom, I imagine, does their poetry get them into difficulties. Beauty and lyricism are really related to another world, to ivory towers, to your head in the cloud, feet floating off the earth. . . . So goes the life of a social poet. I am sure none of these things would ever have happened to me had I limited the subject matter of my poems to roses and moonlight. But, unfortunately, I was born poor—and colored—and almost all the prettiest roses I have seen have been in rich white people's yards—not in mine. That is why I cannot write exclusively about roses and moonlight—for sometimes in the moonlight my brothers see a fiery cross and a circle of Klansmen's hoods. Sometimes in the moonlight a dark body swings from a lynching tree—but for this funeral there are no roses. (205, 212)

The distinction that Hughes makes between "social" or "political" poets and "other poets" who write about the natural world is a fraught one. Hughes's fears are certainly valid. What is also important to note, though, is that this distinction is precisely why New Negro Renaissance poets like Spencer were often dismissed for writing poetry that summoned natural world imagery. Similar to Hughes's critiques, writing about the natural world was considered trite and certainly not a place through which Blackness or the Black political struggle could be rendered. And, like Phillis Wheatley, sometimes they were accused of trying to imitate white writers. Indeed, 1947 was certainly a terrifying time, but so were the 1920s. Spencer reimagined the natural world as a space that was harmonious with Blackness, and her garden-salon allowed her to materialize her vision and share it with close friends and colleagues. Perhaps this is what her friends and colleagues admired so much and why they frequented her home-garden literary salon; they accepted her invitation to imagine, and they saw her garden as an archive of imagination. This decentering of trauma is what makes her garden sacred. She reimagined, re-visioned what the natural world could be for Black people and herself, so in this way, Spencer's garden is not just antidominion; it is also anticolonial.

Spencer learned the art of gardening in the same way that she learned to write poetry: she was a self-taught artist. Her archive is filled with clippings from such gardening resources as *Dreer's Garden Book,* suggesting that she drew inspiration from avid reading as well. Frischkorn and Rainey aptly refer to Spencer as a "self-taught designer" (29), and this designation is important because, in addition to honing her craft, she was also *inventing* a craft of her own. In addition to being a self-taught horticulturalist, she was also a self-taught botanist who crossbred her own plants and may have even crossbred a black poppy.[4] Her garden was filled with plants that she and Edward would collect on their regular, hours-long Sunday-afternoon drives. Indeed, Spencer's use of wild plants is illustrative of how she made ingenious use of the materials available to her, but it also demonstrates her scientific mind at work, a mind that was at ease in the realm of experimentation. What I want to note about Spencer's garden is that it was curated with intention. I read her garden as a quilt in the sense that it was carefully and deliberately assembled with multilayered, multisensory "patches," so to speak, that uniquely reflected her. From the Prince Ebo statue that W. E. B. Du Bois gifted her to her writing cottage, Edankraal, Spencer's garden was a reflection of her and was truly half her world. Her archive at the University of Virginia also reflects this kind of quilting, as what and how Spencer wrote reveal what she held sacred as well as the inextricable link between her writing and love of the natural world. Indeed, one cannot separate her from her garden, and one certainly cannot separate her poetry from her garden because her garden *was* her poetry.

The importance of cultivating one's own pleasure is evident in Spencer's writing process. Spencer wrote for her own enjoyment and edification, and she never considered her writing to be complete. Her archive is rich with drafts of poems that she continued to edit until her death. "Any Wife to Any Husband" is one such poem that Spencer edited throughout her life, and based on the materials available in her archive, it could possibly hold the distinction of being one of her most frequently revised poems. It is not a coincidence that both Spencer's gardening and her writing were daily practices that spanned over seventy years (Frischkorn and Rainey 27). Spencer's attention to cultivation, as evidenced by this poem, in particular, is a testament to the centrality of self-fashioned joy and pleasure in her life. However, Spencer does not shy away from lamenting the difficulties of such cultivation, as evident in the lines from "[Earth, I thank you]," in which she notes the "hard times" and "grunting thru the noun" (Greene 197). Through her garden, Spencer invokes a rich tradition of African American women's strategies for community and individual survival. By encouraging Black women to continue this tradition of gardening, which is both a symbolic and literal act of nurturing, Spencer is articulating the importance of both joy and self-care in one's life; she is encouraging women to nurture themselves and cultivate their own spaces in which they may find joy and happiness.

In offering these diverse possibilities for Black women, Spencer also implicitly engages the prominent New Negro woman rhetoric that cast Black women as "race mothers" whose devotion to racial uplift extinguished the opportunity for self-determinism. These limitations are seen in the essay "The Task of Negro Womanhood," by Elise Johnson McDougald. For McDougald, the New Negro woman exists for everyone except herself and lives in a perpetual state of self-denial: "We find the Negro woman, figuratively struck in the face daily by contempt from the world about her. Within her soul, she knows little of peace and happiness. But through it all, she is courageously standing erect, developing within herself the moral strength to rise above and conquer false attitudes. She is maintaining her natural beauty and charm and improving her mind and opportunity. She is measuring up to the needs of her family, community and race, and radiating a hope throughout the land" (382).

In an untitled, undated draft of a novel, Spencer opens with a woman addressing her husband: "Jerry, I want to be what I've never been, I want to be happy. Surely happiness is the primary right of every human creature."[5] Indeed, Spencer believed it was the primary right of every human creature. By insisting that Black women have the right to joy, happiness, and self-fulfillment, Spencer challenges New Negro patriarchy and undermines the above New Negro woman rhetoric and creates possibilities for the emergence of the pluralities of New Negro *women*. Historian Erin D. Chapman illustrates how Black female writers like Jessie Redmon Fauset, Nella Larsen, and Marita Bonner utilized the "domestic sphere" of writing and wrote fiction that allowed them to "explore the unspeakable, that which they did not or could not incorporate into New Negro politics," and how through writing Black women were able to express both their wholeness and sexual self-determination (133). These Black female writers often concluded what Elise Johnson McDougald espoused—that there was little happiness to be found—so they turned to their fiction writing to both explore and articulate possibilities beyond the realm of perpetual unhappiness and self-denial. Chapman explains that for Larsen and Fauset, in particular, "the question of happiness" was central to their work, and they created female protagonists who were sexually liberated and did not settle for a partnership that lacked respect and joy (141, 142). Noticeably absent from Chapman's analysis (as well as other analyses on New Negro women writers' resistance) is Anne Spencer, for whom the ideas of the "New Negro woman" and "happiness" are not only a possibility but also inextricably linked. Spencer was also acutely aware of the masculinist, patriarchal orientation of the New Negro movement, and though she utilized her writing to challenge these norms much like her contemporaries, Spencer's discursive strategies often relied on her own personal views and personal life, not fictional representations. Thus, for Spencer, the personal was political.

Spencer's use of her personal sentiments as a political, discursive strategy is evident in the poem "He Said:":

"Your garden at dusk
Is the soul of love
Blurred in its beauty
And softly caressing;
I, gently daring
This sweetest confessing,
Say your garden at dusk
Is your soul, My Love." (Greene 183)

In this poem, Spencer writes about her husband's feelings both for her and her garden, and what we see in this poem is confirmation of the statement, "This small garden is half my world." The speaker says, "your garden at dusk/Is your soul, My Love" (Greene 183). This assertion is more than a lover's musing because with this statement, Spencer both challenges the masculinist rhetoric of New Negro womanhood and articulates Black environmental consciousness. We can read "He Said:" alongside "Any Wife to Any Husband" as an ongoing conversation about gender equality. In "Any Wife to Any Husband" Spencer asserts that it is a Black woman's right to joy and happiness, and here in "He Said:", Edward Spencer, her husband, not only supports this claim for individuality, but he *repeats* it.

Read in this context, these poems operate as a call and response. Notice that Spencer does not mention matrimony in this poem. The title is simple: "He Said:", not "My Husband Said" or "Edward Said." The title's simplicity almost assumes a flippant quality, and we are to understand that "he" is her husband, Edward. The move to not use her husband's name or the word "husband" echoes the sentiments in "Any Wife to Any Husband": that her world and her womanhood are more expansive than the confines of matrimony, and Edward's statement in the poem affirms this. "He Said:" can be read as Edward's affirming his wife's individuality and her right to pursue her own happiness separate from him and outside of prescriptive notions of the domestic sphere.

Edward played an integral role in the garden, and the garden was significant to the Spencers' marriage. Edward built the garden for his wife, and the couple would often travel long distances in search of plants and horticultural accouterments to add to the garden. He helped her take care of the garden and cultivate it, and it "remained a relic of the love bond between Anne and Edward" (Greene 110). He also built her writing cottage, Edankraal, whose name is derived from Anne's and Edward's first names and the Afrikaans word "kraal," meaning "dwelling" or "corral." The couple often gardened together by moonlight, so the poem's reference to gardening at "dusk" is an autobiographical reference. By offering Edward's intimate thoughts, Anne Spencer challenges the notion that New Negro womanhood is predicated on self-denial and illustrates that an egalitarian relationship can exist in reality, not just in the fictional writings of Larsen and Fauset, and the garden itself becomes a symbol of an egalitarian relationship.

What we also see in this poem is an articulation of a Black man's environmental consciousness, and in this articulation, Spencer not only gestures to the reader that the natural world is accessible to Black men, but also she utilizes Edward's words to debunk myths about Black sexuality. As mentioned above, Spencer invokes the long-standing tradition of gardening and its significance to African American women. By including Edward's words, she invokes both his role in cultivating the garden as well as his environmental consciousness, and she demonstrates that the natural world is not gender exclusive and can be accessed by both Black men and women alike. Furthermore, Edward's words about Anne are profoundly loving and intimate; however, he does not mention her corporeal body, and this love poem, though erotic, is not sexual in nature. That Edward speaks about his Black wife in nonphysical, nonsexual terms and instead speaks of her soul, challenges the pervasive notion that Black women and Black female sexuality are inherently transgressive. This "decorporealizing" of the Black female body and emphasizing the soul or the mind is a strategy of bodily representation that many writers turned to in the nineteenth century in attempt to reclaim the "eccentric" Black body; thus, Spencer is summoning a long-standing tradition of African American rhetorical resistance in writing about these specific words her husband spoke to her (Peterson, "Foreword" xii). Through this act, Edward symbolically inscribes new meaning into Black women's bodies, and by associating Black women with the environment, Edward writes a new narrative about Black female sexuality and claims that both Black women's bodies and their sexuality are *natural,* not transgressive. By calling the reader's attention to Anne's soul, Edward is not only saying that there is more to his wife than her physicality; he is also saying that his wife and all Black women are *human* and should be appreciated and acknowledged as human beings, not just bodies and flesh. Furthermore, that Edward, as a Black male, privileges the nonphysical aspects of his wife and does not speak about her in a sexual manner provides a counternarrative to myths about Black male hypersexuality and lasciviousness. Thus, in this poem, Spencer uses her personal relationships with Edward and the natural world as powerful political counternarratives.

Critics have contended that Spencer's poetry lacks a strong racial orientation; however, Spencer's poetry is inextricably linked to her lived experience as a Black woman, and her discursive strategies and poetic choices reveal that the intersections of her identity as a Black woman were infused in her writing. It is when we juxtapose Spencer's environmental consciousness with her positionality as a Black woman that we the ways in which Spencer's work engages and responds to myths and stereotypes concerning African Americans and their relationship to the environment. Spencer's nature poems correct and revise the misconception that the natural world is a "white space," and she offers a uniquely Black, female environmental aesthetic that also challenges dominant tropes about Black women's bodies. When Spencer's rhetorical contributions are unearthed, what emerges is a rhetoric of Black womanhood predicated on individuality, self-care, and happiness, a rhetoric that appropriately locates her as a key forerunner to Black feminist writers. Though Spencer's body of work is underutilized and misunderstood, the juxtaposition of her environmental consciousness and ideas of Black womanhood reveals that through her work, she both corrected and resisted pervasive racist narratives and created apertures through which subsequent Black writers could both articulate their environmental consciousness and reclaim and recast Black women's bodies. Spencer's affinity for the natural world may have cost her publication success in the conventional sense, but her ability to reimagine and revision the symbolism of the natural world and use it as a generative space underscore the magnitude of her imagination and theoretical savvy. By sharing "half her world," Spencer's poetry is an invitation to expand the contours of our imagination.

3

"God Never Planted a Garden"

Anne Spencer's Ecotheology

"I know my soul to be sinful, but I believe it to be honest. I believe that if I had all, instead of some, of the blood my distant grandsire gave me I'd refuse to be a hater of man. The hate-type of person who loves a dog because it so perfectly establishes his own human superiority."[1] Here, Spencer is signaling her mixed-race ancestry, as she is of white, Black, and Seminole Indian heritage. She is perhaps directly referring to her maternal grandfather, whom she described to her biographer as "a wealthy Virginia aristocrat" (Greene 4). Spencer penned these words in one of her many notebooks that housed her writings and private thoughts. I begin this chapter with this quote for two reasons. First, it signals that Spencer possessed a theology that was central to her ontological theorizing. Second, this quote is emblematic of the fact that her theology was one that she fashioned on her own, and it was grounded in an antidominion ecology that expressed reverence for human and nonhuman nature. Though Spencer was not religious, her poetry and archive reveal an intimate spirituality and that she indeed believed in a God. Just as with publication and her vision for her garden, her aversion toward confinement and containment extended to her conception of God. In the same notebook a few pages away from the above quote, she writes, "Definition is man's weakest trap for catching God, to catch and confine."[2]

This chapter extends my analysis of Spencer's ecopoetics and seeks to understand both Spencer's (re)visioning and conception of God *in relation* to the natural world. Though this chapter is concerned with Spencer's theology, it is equally concerned with her ecological consciousness because, for

Spencer, God was of nature, and nature was of God. Whereas chapter 2 ana-lyzed how the natural world gave Spencer the poetics to create poetry and prose, this chapter is concerned with how the natural world enabled her to create and reimagine God. What I mean by this is that I am interested in the God that Spencer creates as well why she summons natural world idioms to create her God. Like her carefully crafted garden and archive, Spencer's God was also a deliberate construction and reimagining. This reimagining is evi-dent in the aforementioned quote, as Spencer critiques notions of dominion and anthropocentrism. Spencer tacitly critiques traditional Christian beliefs of sin that would exclude dominion and anthropocentrism as sinful acts, and by alluding to her (white) grandsire, she suggests that the sins of racism and exploitation of the natural world are inextricably linked. The critiques in her above quote mirror the womanist theology of such scholars as Delores S. Williams and Shamara Shantu Riley, who argue that the assaults upon the natural world and Black women's bodies are the same sin.[3]

As I noted in the introduction, one of the aims of this book is to establish Spencer as an unsung cultural theorist and early environmentalist. My refer-ence to womanism, ecowomanism, and womanist theology here is not to align Spencer's personal politics with womanist epistemology, as such language was not available to Spencer.[4] This work positions natural world writings as a hallmark and legacy of Black women's theoretical savviness and creativity; thus, my reference to these epistemological traditions is my attempt to trace a kind of intellectual history and locate Spencer as a key progenitor. Because of her civil rights activism and appreciation for the natural world, Spencer's the-ology anticipates both theological womanism and what is now called Black environmental liberation theology (BELT), making her writings historically significant, timely, and urgent.[5] Dianne D. Glave explains BELT as follows:

Black liberation theology, which decries the oppression of African Americans based on biblical principles—is the foundation of BELT, a nascent theology based on environmental justice history and activism by African American Christians. Like black liberation theology, BELT is both a theology and an ideology that is actualized by shielding con-temporary African Americans exposed to toxins and pollution from landfills, garbage dumps, auto mechanics' shops, and sewage plants.... The language of theology is a means of combating environmental rac-ism. Black liberation theology is based on scriptures, especially from the New Testament, that hold the promise of environmental equity and justice for African Americans. ("Black Environmental" 190)

I also draw upon Glave's definition and historicizing of "ecotheology," as she distinguishes between white Christian ecotheology and an African and Black ecotheology that is rooted in liberation theology and BELT. Glave's comprehensive definition takes into account how Black individuals have had to work to reimagine not only Christianity and God but also the natural world and that they have had to contend with the weight of double consciousness in nature, a phenomenon Kimberly N. Ruffin refers to as the "ecological burden-and-beauty-paradox" that positions Black people as "ecological pariahs" (2, 16).[6] Such reimagining allows nature to be "treated and celebrated as a sacrament, a Christian ritual like baptism or communion" (Glave, "Eco-Theology" 88). I refer to Spencer's theology as "ecotheology" to underscore that, for Spencer, nature was divine and the divine could be found in the natural world. Spencer did not separate herself from her garden especially in her spirituality, and her conception of God reveals as much about her spirituality as it does about her relationship to the natural world. I intentionally use "ecotheology" as opposed to a more specific term such as "ecoreligion" or "eco-Christianity" because, while Spencer's archive suggests that she was deeply spiritual, it does not suggest that she was religious or denominationally Christian. What it does suggest, however, is that her spirituality was predicated upon the natural world. Perhaps the closest she comes to articulating religious affiliation is in her biographical note in *Caroling Dusk* in which she writes, "I am a Christian by intention, a Methodist by inheritance, and a Baptist by marriage" (qtd. in Cullen 47). Greene remarks that she "was certainly one of Lynchburg's most vocal and active social heretics" (98), so it is possible that she was vocal about her religious views, as she was with her political views. She was very critical of religion in her private writings and took issue with the desire to "trap" and "confine" God. That being said, she attended church regularly with her family. Because she was so active in her community, it is also possible that the regular church attendance reflects her desire to stay connected to the close-knit Lynchburg community.

Indeed, Spencer's appropriation and reimagining of God and Christianity are illustrative of a long-standing tradition within African American history, literature, culture, and Black feminist and womanist writing, more specifically. Religion was integral to enslaved individuals' survival; however, it is important not to confuse "religion" with "Christianity" because, as Michael Gomez explains, "it is much more likely that African religions were still practiced by a majority, with some transformation of meaning, along with the incorporation of a few tenets of the Christian faith" well into the second decade of the nineteenth century (256). This "transformed" version of Euro-Christianity fused with African religions is a crucial example of a means of survival enslaved people developed and demonstrates that they wrested control from their white enslavers and "conquered the religion of those who conquered them" (Genovese 212). Adopting what is now called liberation theology, enslaved individuals created a worldview for themselves predicated on refashioned images of God and Jesus (free of paternalistic, punitive overtones) as their personal intercessors and deliverers and strongly identified with the enslaved children of Israel. Christianity was also of particular significance to enslaved women, and because of their previously noted vulnerability to sexual violence, enslaved women were drawn to Jesus Christ and developed an "unfathomable faith" and identified with his suffering and persecution on an intimate level, with many enslaved women feeling that "Jesus was their last refuge" (Collier-Thomas 10, 12). That religion played such an integral role in shaping the worldview of enslaved people while in bondage explains why, as Leon Litwack notes, the Black church would become "the central and unifying institution in the postwar black community" far more than any organization (471).

This chapter draws upon Elizabeth J. West's study of African and Christian spiritual poetics in Black women's literature in *African Spirituality in Black Women's Fiction* (2011) and Tomeiko Ashford Carter's examination of Black women's spiritual autobiographies in *Powers Divine* (2009). West and Carter name spiritual writing as a part of Black women's ontological theorizing and identify the following unique patterns in their appropriation and articulation of the divine and religion.[7] West delineates these patterns as:

> 1) the value of memory to both individual and group well-being; 2) the belief that community represents the essence of human existence and being; 3) the view that nature—both animate and inanimate—represents divineness; and 4) belief in the interconnectedness of worldly and otherworldly beings. These principles are integral to black epistemological and ontological thought, pre–and post–Middle Passage and are central to shaping a tradition of spiritual exploration in black women's writing. African American women writers from Wheatley to Morrison integrate these themes in their work, signaling the early maintenance and integration of an African worldview among displaced Africans and the important role of women as carriers of culture. (19)

Similar to West, Carter's examination of spiritual autobiographies identifies defining characteristics of Black women writers' spiritual writing, noting how their writing is a reimagining of divine agency and divine power: "Modern authors express divine agency more audaciously as ontological ideologies, or modes of every day existence. That is, contemporary (black female) writers expand the function of divine power in their fiction" (xvi).[8] Though I do not intend to argue that Spencer's (re)visioning of God is Africanist or suggests an articulation of an African worldview, I do want to call attention to the ways her theorizing deviates from traditional, Western conceptions of God and the natural world and might be inspired by non-Western thought. I draw upon West's and Carter's work to illustrate that such reimagining is endemic to Black women's poetics and Black women's ontological theorizing. Both West and Carter center their studies in the genre of spiritual autobiographies, so I also extend their analyses by foregrounding Spencer's poetry and nonfiction prose. Spencer's archive is a rich case study because it contains poetry and prose both published and unpublished. Therefore, I can position her as unsung real-life "divine heroine" (xix), a term Carter uses to describe the female protagonists in the spiritual autobiographies she examines, who struggled daily to fashion and maintain a theology that enabled her to *be*.

There is something ritualistic about Spencer's eccentric daily routine of rising midmorning and spending the entire afternoon, evening, and early morning writing and communing with her garden that I referenced in chapter 1. While I acknowledge that the optics of a Black woman tending to the natural world conjures images associated with enslavement and coercive labor, I intentionally use the word "communing" to describe her engagement with her garden because she did not consider her gardening to be labor. The word "labor" connotes economics and the production of goods for wages and thus becomes a difficult word to use with regard to Black women who have a fraught history of neither being able to exercise autonomous control over their bodies and labor. The word "commune" denotes intimate communication, and this is the essence of Spencer's relationship with the natural world ("commune").[9]

Spencer's need for and insistence upon solitude is a cultivation of her spiritual self, and bell hooks notes that it is in these rare, precious moments of solitude that Black women are able to cultivate the divine: "Taking time to experience ourselves in solitude is one way we that we can regain a sense of the divine that can feel the spirit moving in our lives. Solitude is essential to the spiritual for it is there that we can not only commune with divine spirits but also listen to our inner voice" (*Sisters of the Yam* 143). Taken as a part of her theological praxis, however, this eccentricity is a restructuring and redefining of the divine, one that is circular in structure and nonhierarchical. This circular structure as well as Spencer's spirituality and self-care is akin to Alice Walker's definition of womanism (*Mothers' Gardens* xii). Her relationship to her garden is a symbiotic, reciprocal relationship in which she would tend her plants, and they would inspire her poetics and spiritual well-being, which is something carefully noted by her biographer:

> For a woman whose mental and spiritual selves were not in harmony with her human environment, her garden was a palliative haven. In Lynchburg it became her "last comfort in Gethsemane" as she sought spiritual shelter from the town's hostile society. . . . Such a withdrawal was not so much to escape her family, but when she retired to the garden house she was freed from living the traditionally exact roles of mother and wife. She needed and desired a certain spiritual nourishment which her family and friends could not provide her, and which she found in her garden world of nature. (Greene 108–9)

Notice what Greene says about Spencer: that her "mental and spiritual selves were not in harmony with her *human* environment" and that her garden provided a "spiritual shelter." Greene is signaling that in nature Spencer was able to realize something in herself that was not possible in society—something that is akin to the profound wholeness and subjectivity Audre Lorde describes as the erotic, which she has called "a measure between the beginnings of our sense of self and the chaos of our strongest feelings. It is an internal sense of satisfaction to which, once we have experienced it, we know we can aspire" (*Sister Outsider* 54). Greene alludes to the very important fact that Spencer lived in Lynchburg and consequently was at the mercy of Jane Crow, so part of this spiritual sheltering that her natural world provided was also a shelter from the color line. I want to recall the fact that Spencer moved away from utilitarianism in relation to her garden because just as with her writing, her garden served as a kind of blueprint for her life, especially her theology. The communal relationship Greene describes is actually something much more profound. The reason why the natural world is a source of spirituality for Spencer is because she is able to locate the divine within it, and, as a result, she is able to identify and cultivate the divine within herself.

Once again, I turn to Alice Walker's *In Search of Our Mothers' Gardens* and heed Walker's imperative to both look for and honor the "creative sparks" with which Black women live their lives (240). Walker asks: "What did it mean for a black woman to be an artist in our grandmothers' time? In our great-grandmothers' day?" (233). For Spencer, born only one generation after slavery and living in the Lynchburg, Virginia, the answer to this question was indeed "cruel enough to stop the blood" (Walker 233). Spencer is a Creator, but unlike the grandmothers and mothers Walker describes, she was not "driven to a numb and bleeding madness by the springs of creativity in them for which there was no release," and she did not live a life of "spiritual waste" (233). This chapter bears witness to Spencer's theological creativity and honors her audacity to create her own God and theology, and to identify and cultivate the divine within herself. In saying that Spencer creates her own God, I am not suggesting that Spencer fashioned her own, distinct faith tradition. Spencer's God and theology are deeply informed by Western Protestant Christian faith traditions, and her concept of God is drawn from the Hebrew God. Rather, I am interested in how she re-visions God as she does with the natural world. Spencer loved being a Black woman, perhaps more than anything else, and her love of her Black womanhood is articulated in published and unpublished writings with some iteration of the phrase, "I proudly love being a Negro woman," appearing repeatedly (qtd. in Cullen 47). Chapter 1 argues that Spencer's "'leventy-leven bits" were constructions of a Black woman's world, and here I extend this argument by suggesting that Spencer created a Black woman's God, one that enabled to love herself. One of the questions in relation to Spencer that I am often asked is some iteration of "why." *Why did Spencer write about the natural world? Why did she write on ephemera? Why did she not publish her writings?* While versions of these "why?" questions have certainly sparked my research, I think the more appropriate question to ask about Spencer's theology is not why but "what?" Thus, this chapter seeks to understand Spencer's transformation of God, namely *what* Spencer's God and theology looked like and *what* this creation enabled her to do. Georgia Douglas Johnson did not separate Spencer from her "garden, . . . elegant verse, and . . . sure philosophy," and in this chapter, I want to discuss the nuances of her sure philosophy to demonstrate that, for Spencer, her writing, womanhood, theology, and the natural world were inextricably linked.[10]

I feel moved to pause here for a moment and honor the fact that Spencer was audacious enough and thought enough of herself to imagine the God that she both needed and wanted. Like her use of "'leventy-leven," it is certainly a testament to her improvisational energy and inventiveness, but, more importantly, it is a testament to the fact that she loved herself so much that she cultivated and nurtured a divine self-love during a time when Black womanhood was defiled. During a time and in a world in which her Black female body was told where to fit, she created a God that fit *her*. And it was good.

Many of Spencer's poems are infused with natural world imagery, but I want to first focus on an unpublished, undated, handwritten manuscript entitled "Love and Gardens" because it beautifully illustrates how the poetics of the natural world enabled her to articulate herself. Spencer's meditations on motherhood and parenting are also revealed in this essay, and she opens the essay with an anecdote, recalling a quote from a garden manual that perplexed her, which reads, "Flowers grow for those who love them and the secret of success is in the worker" (qtd. in "Love and Gardens," 1).[11] In response to this quote, Spencer is compelled to ask, "What are flowers and where are gardens?" It is this question that sparks the essay, and though the quote originated from a garden manual, Spencer uses the analogy of gardening to theorize the God-human, parent-child relationship:

> Our Lord is the great Gardener, Parents are his undergardeners[.] Children are the flowers. "And flowers bloom for those who love them and the secret of success is in the worker." This Tiny circle called the family is the unit of all that is good or bad in the world. Parents must instill into their children the peaceful civilization of the next hundred years[.] If we hate war & love peace, desire pure government for the masses, If we desire brave spirits and dauntless hearts that can live above prejudice and wrong[,] Let us train our children with a tedious care for little things—train them born & unborn.... And, too, parents if there is one thing more than another we are doing it is forcing our flowers in a hot house; when all out of doors in God's sturdy wind & golden sunshine is the place for them to grow. ("Love and Gardens" 4–6)

This excerpt reveals several important things about Spencer's mediations on parenting, but, more importantly, it tells us about the God that Spencer imagines and the womanhood that is possible because of it. Spencer's garden (and the act of gardening itself) was indeed the lens through which she viewed all aspects of her life. That she likens parenting to being a gardener reveals that her garden occupies an intimate space in her consciousness, one that enables her to make meaning of herself and the world around her. This analogy illustrates that the natural world not only provided her with freedom and poetics to theorize her womanhood; the natural world was also a generative space that enabled her to theorize in general. As previously noted, gardening was a form of creative expression for Spencer that allowed her the space to experiment and improvise; it was to be celebrated for its beauty, not consumed. Spencer's garden was a celebration of her individuality and imaginative prowess, so this analogy reveals that she views parenting as a means through which one cultivates individuality. Spencer invites us to locate nature as a site of Black feminist spiritual writing. In doing so, Spencer offers another way to think about how Black women articulate their womanhood and their spirituality. Spencer incorporates theology in her theorizing and names God as the "the Great Gardener." Though Spencer acknowledges divine ordination in the human–natural world relationship, notice that her understanding deviates from notions of dominion. She imagines God as a gardener, one who cultivates and entrusts human beings with the task of "undergardening," which is an act of cultivating, not ruling. Spencer's caution against "forcing our flowers in a hot house" also functions as a critique of dominion, as she argues that children-flowers need to grow unencumbered.

Spencer demonstrates her spiritual agency and creativity by imagining God as a gardener. Implicit in the above excerpt is that this is the God that Spencer desires. Spencer does not walk us through a transformation of God from "old white man" to gardener as Shug Avery does in *The Color Purple* (195), but Spencer's tone tells us this transformation has already taken place, and this God is her creation. "Love and Gardens" could be renamed "The Gospel According to Anne Spencer" because it functions as a parable giving us insight into Spencer's theology and her conceptions of the divine. In the same way that the natural world is her poetic muse, it is also her spiritual muse, so it is fitting that Spencer's God would be a "the Great Gardener." Her tone is assertive, authoritative, and knowing. In true Gospel form, Spencer is teaching, she is telling, and she is revealing. Spencer is not speaking in metaphor or using similes here. She is not telling us what God is like. She is telling us precisely who God *is*, and he is a gardener. In telling us who and what her God is, she is also telling us what he is not, so the above excerpt (and the document as a whole) functions as a corrective account of God, and she is writing against Western conceptions of God. By insisting upon a God who is of the natural world, Spencer is not only able to locate the natural world as a divine space; she also is able to posit her Black womanhood (and the theory that it produces) as natural and destabilize conventional notions of what is natural. She establishes her own Holy Trinity, which consists of Black womanhood, nature, and God.

What is at stake here is not just what Spencer is telling us about God but also what Spencer is telling us about herself. That she positions herself as a kind of prophet and disciple tells us that Spencer believes that she has the *right* to speak about God, and the tenor of her prose suggests that she feels it is imperative. What Spencer communicates is that she views herself as divine, which is a radical reframing of Black women's bodies.[12] Thus, in this Gospel according to Spencer, she is redefining what it means to be divine. She is also telling us that she, as a Black woman, is divine (and therefore Black women are divine) and Black women's knowledge production is divine. But Spencer's audacity does not stop with her speaking about God. She sees God as "the Great Gardener" arguably because she is a gardener herself. In other words, she creates God in her own image. So she not only envisions a Black woman's God, but she also envisions God as a Black woman or, more specifically, as a being who *could* be a Black woman. I want to comment briefly on Spencer's theorizing of male gender here because she is doing something quite provocative. Spencer regularly genders God as male in her writings, so my intention here is not to state that Spencer viewed God as a Black woman and only a Black woman. She is theorizing maleness in way that is not oppositional to Black womanhood, and I am reminded of Hortense Spillers's statement in "Mama's Baby, Papa's Maybe": "It is the heritage of the *mother* that the African-American male must regain as an aspect of his own personhood—the power of 'yes' to the 'female' within" (80; emphasis original). Though Spencer genders her God as male, there is an acknowledgment of the female within. What I am suggesting here is that her creating a God after her own image implies that she allows for the possibility that God could be a Black woman. More specifically, this fluidity is consistent with her aversion toward containment and underscores her aforementioned critique of man trapping and confining God. By creating a God that is *of* herself, Spencer engages in what I term an *embodied ecotheology* because this is a God that exists because of Spencer's Black womanhood and is rendered through her Black womanhood. Just as her archive is more than a collection of her writings and is also an archive of her and her emotions, Spencer's God functions in the same way and is a piece of her. In my use of *embodied ecotheology*, I am informed by Brittney Cooper's term "embodied discourse," discussed in chapter 1. In the same way that Cooper argues that Anna Julia Cooper "fundamentally believed that we cannot divorce Black women's bodies from the theory they produce" (3), I affirm this analysis by highlighting how Spencer centered herself in her knowledge production.

That Spencer imagines God as a gardener signals her intimate relationship with the natural world, but it also underscores her aversion to containment and confinement. Even though Spencer is precise about God's role as gardener, recall from chapter 1 that gardening can signify the work of art of a gardener and is not limited to horticulture. Thus, her statement, "Our Lord is the great Gardener," could be rewritten as, "Our Lord is the great Artist." The God that Spencer imagines is an artist who tasks individuals with "undergardening," or creating art. In using the language of parenting and playing with conceptions of the Holy Trinity Godhead, namely "God the Father," she beautifully deconstructs these conventional notions and instead erects "God the Artist." In this Gospel, Spencer is telling the reader that because God is an artist, he cultivates other artists. In this way, the antidominion critique is also an insistence on the individual-artist's right to creative expression, which Spencer is positioning as a divine right. The familial structure described is essentially an artists' utopia with a God who allows her to be an artist and be of her art. Thus, in addition to theorizing alternative parenting styles, Spencer offers a new way of *being* for Black women, one that allows them the possibility of imagining and creating a Black woman's world with a God who cultivates them and encourages both self-cultivation and the cultivation of others. In this way, Spencer creates a God who not only allows but encourages her to love herself and her artistry. Perhaps the most vital intervention that Spencer's Gospel makes is that God does have to be singular and stagnant. By envisioning a God who is an artist cultivating other artists, she also creates an implicit invitation for individuals to imagine God on their own terms.

Spencer's creating a God in her own image and affirming her divinity is a powerful reclamation and rewriting of female spirituality, one that is also grounded in self-love. This rewriting is not unique to Spencer and has a long-standing Black feminist tradition. Audre Lorde's theory of the erotic as "the nurturer of or nursemaid of all our deepest knowledge" locates female spirituality as a source of intellect (*Sister Outsider* 56). In Ntozake Shange's choreopoem *for colored girls,* the lady in red states, "i found god in myself & i loved her/i loved her fiercely" (63). Similarly, literary critic Maha Marouan argues in *Witches, Goddesses, and Angry Spirits* that Toni Morrison writes Black female spirituality in a way that is liberatory and embraces female power: "Morrison constructs a specific model of spirituality that challenges the nature of the male god in Judeo-Christianity as wholly good and masculine, evoking archetypal goddesses, ambivalent in character" (75).[13] By calling attention to how such writers as Ntozake

Shange, Audre Lorde, and Toni Morrison have affirmed the divine Black woman, I want to signal how Spencer is, in fact, in line with—and continued—a legacy of Black women's spiritual writing practices.

One of the recurring themes in Spencer's writing about God is a critique of humans' misunderstanding of God as a being who can be contained and understood. Her unpublished, handwritten poem entitled "The Adviser" highlights the unfounded assumptions humans make about God:

> He had let me speak to Him about
> The straight line:
> "God," I said, this line is going out Too far. Turn it.
> Straight lines are hollow and
> Empty—They hold nothing—
> Child, He said and softly [—]once
> when I was older we had been too
> near each other and he scolded with Thunder[—]
> Your impinging little mind [is] limited
> This is no straight line
> But curved in Time not in space [—] its reach is eons before
> Your sight and eons after[.][14]

This poem is accompanied by the date "December 1970," so it is possible that it was written around this time just five years before her death. It may hold the distinction of being one of the few poems that Spencer dated herself. However, as I mentioned in chapter 1, Spencer's archive contains its own logics, so this date may not correspond to the date when the poem was actually written. This is a poem in which a powerful transformation takes place, and I want to focus on the speaker of this poem because the powerful transformation takes place within her, and it is both implied and subtle. The poem is rich with a playfulness and sarcasm that is seen in the reference to the stereotypical authoritative God who scolds with thunder. However, this poem is also very solemn and reverent because, by the end of the poem, a profound shift has taken place both within the speaker, namely in how she perceives herself, and in how God is characterized. The poem begins with Spencer's audacious speaker confronting God about a "straight line," which is a metaphor rife with ambiguity. God engages her plea but corrects her, letting her know that the straight line is actually a curved one. Notice that God corrects the speaker with what might be considered an insult and says that her "impinging little mind [is] limited." I want to pause here for a moment and talk about this phrase because it is not an insult; rather, it is a warning with an implicit invitation. The speaker's mind is not "little" by nature in the sense that it is ill-equipped or incapable. It is "little" because it is impinging, and here I must note that God seems to be invoking the definition of "impinge" that means "encroach" or "infringe."[15]

The warning that God provides to the speaker is that she is limiting herself and if she continues to be impinging, she will be unable to see curved lines. Notice how God carefully explains and qualifies the curved line: it is curved in time and not in space, and its reach is eons before *her sight* and eons after. Once again, God points to the limitations of the speaker's sight (arguably caused by her "impinging little mind"). In calling attention to her limitations, he implicitly invites her to move outside of her narrow mind-set. Assuming that the speaker is a Black woman like Spencer, the "straight line" could easily be read as metonym for Black women's oppressions and the prescriptive gender roles thrust upon them and evokes iterations of the colloquialism "walk the straight and narrow." However, Spencer's speaker seems to hold misconceptions about both God and herself, and this "straight line" instead is a metaphor for her linear, utilitarian thinking. The speaker reveals her utilitarian mode of thinking in her complaint about the straight line when she says that it is "hollow" and "holds nothing." In other words, her frustration is not truly with the shape of the line; it is that the line is not useful to her and cannot be manipulated to her liking. Its straightness prevents it from being useful *to her*.

To further unpack this poem and the powerful transformation that takes place, we must understand the nature of the speaker's misconceptions that are certainly fueled by her mind-set. The speaker confronts God *assuming* not only that he created the straight line but also that he is responsible for fixing it. In telling her that the line is curved, God is telling that speaker that she misunderstands *him* and misunderstands *herself*. Thus, what God is saying here is, "I did not create this straight line. You did." Implied in the speaker's confrontation is that her image of God is one that is like the straight line she detests so much because she believes in a utilitarian God who can "fix" and "turn" the line for her because she *also* believes that he is the creator of said straight lines. God corrects her, and, in doing so, he also informs the speaker that she has also been wrong about him. If we juxtapose this God with the God Spencer depicts in "Love and Gardens," what God is telling the speaker here is that he is an artist, not an authoritarian and not a utilitarian. Through his critique of her "impinging little mind," he also informs her that it is her responsibility to fix the straight line, not his. And here we see a beautiful demonstration of Spencer's theorizing because she has created a God who insists on individuals' spiritual agency and responsibility. Notice that God does not provide specifics about the nature of the curved line, but the speaker, on the other hand, informs us of how impractical straight lines are. In other words, God tells the speaker what that the curved line *is,* but he does not tell her what it is *for,* illustrating that he is not an authoritative, utilitarian God. Rather, he is a God who thinks in terms of possibilities, not limitations.

This poem is certainly about the speaker's misunderstanding of God, but it is also about a profound misunderstanding of herself. In his constructive criticism, God is careful to note that the "reach" of the line extends eons before and after *her sight.* This qualification is the most poignant and profound piece of the criticism God provides as he simultaneously communicates precisely who he is and shows her that her "impinging little mind" has rendered her blind. His deliberate use of "your sight," as opposed to "human sight," is specific and nonhierarchical. This statement could be read as condescension and God's assertion of his omniscience, but God's repetitive use of "your" is specific to the speaker, so he is not making a categorical statement about human intellect. By making his critique specific, God is able to reveal himself to the speaker and also reveal the speaker to herself. In addition to implicitly saying that he did not create the straight line, God also tells the speaker that she has been wrong not only about him but also about *her own* capabilities. Thus, God's statement to the speaker could be written as, "Child, you are divine." God's affectionate use of "Child" before he begins his criticism might gesture toward what we now call African American Vernacular English and is Spencer's subtle way of letting the reader know that she is, indeed, imagining a Black God.

The poem is written in the past tense, so the speaker is recalling her former self and her former "impinging little mind." Though the reader is not privy to the internal transformation that takes place, the fact that the speaker is telling her story from a reflective stance suggests that her thought processes have expanded, and she has embraced a "curved-line" thinking. This poem becomes an act of storytelling for the speaker, and this storytelling in poem form becomes a kind of personal testimony of the speaker's spiritual growth and is a manifestation of a "curved line" mentality because it showcases her transformation from "impinging" into artistry. The title of the poem is also a confirmation of the speaker's transformation and suggests that the speaker has been able to make meaning out of her conversation with God. That God is renamed "The Adviser" is also of importance because it signals a significant shift away from the utilitarian God who is supposed to "fix" straight lines; she has reimagined him as a partner, a mentor with whom to dialogue and converse. And, indeed, God is providing counsel in this poem, but his counsel is what frees her. The reader thus bears witness to the speaker's transformation of God from authoritarian to adviser, a being she creates. We must recall that at the core of Spencer's "sure philosophy" is a deliberate move away from utilitarian motives and thinking, stemming from her own personal anxieties about being consumed. Just as with God the Great Gardener, Spencer insists upon an image of God that is expansive and unrestrictive. As noted above, "The Adviser" could have been written in 1970, approximately five years before Spencer passed away, and though I refer to this piece of writing as a poem, I also allow for the possibility that, instead, this is an example of Spencer's creative nonfiction and her summation of her spiritual growth. In other words, this piece of writing could be a semiautobiographical account of her own transformation and how she learned to create God in her own image. Because conversion is at the core of this poem, it evokes biblical motifs just as "Love and Gardens" does. In this way, "The Adviser" becomes a kind of conversion narrative.[16] However, unlike biblical conversion narratives in which the protagonist converts to Christianity after an encounter that demonstrates God's omniscience, Spencer's conversion narrative centers the speaker, and she is not converting to Christianity or fidelity to an outward God. Rather, this conversion is internal, and she is able to identify and cultivate the divine within herself.

As discussed in chapter 1, Spencer's relationship with the natural world is rooted in an antidominion, anticolonial stance. Therefore, the God she envisions must also have the same philosophies. Though Spencer was probably not a religious individual, her spirituality and conception of God were influenced by the Bible, and her archive is filled with her close readings of Bible verses. Most notably, Spencer writes about the significance of Deuteronomy 22:6, which states, "If you come across a bird's nest beside the road, either in a tree or on the ground, and the mother is sitting on the young or on the eggs, do not take the mother with the young" (NIV).[17] "This passage," Spencer writes, "(like other wisdom of the Talmud) was the first S.P.C.A. [Society for the Prevention of Cruelty to Animals] stuff[.] The Earth humanely prohibited the taking away of the brooding bird from her eggs."[18] Spencer's biblically based critique of anthropocentrism and dominion is compelling, especially considering that such critiques were still emergent at the time of her death in 1975. This scriptural close reading also provides further insight into her conception of God, and I want to return to Spencer's opening quote in this chapter and juxtapose it with her scriptural commentary because together they highlight Spencer's critique of dominion. Recall how Spencer characterizes white men: "The hate-type of person who loves a dog because it so perfectly establishes his own human superiority."[19] Spencer's commentary about brooding birds and ill-founded love of dogs reveals more than care for the nonhuman environment. For Spencer, human superiority predicated on and articulated through the exploitation of the natural environment and nonhuman environment constitutes sin and is "unnatural." Spencer, in turn, destabilizes traditional understandings of nature, positioning human superiority (including white supremacy) as an ideology that also defaces the artistry of God, an artistry she celebrates in "Love and Gardens."

This sentiment of the destruction of nature is seen in her posthumously published, untitled poem "[God never planted a garden]":

> God never planted a garden
> But He placed a keeper there;
> And the keeper ever razed the ground
> And built a city where
> God cannot walk at the eve of day,
> Nor take the morning air. (Greene 182)

The brevity and rhyme scheme of the poem give the false illusion of lightheartedness and simplicity. However, this poem is rife with scathing critiques. What Spencer is able to communicate through this poem is illustrative of her imaginative and theoretical prowess. Immediately, there is a dissonance between the form of the poem and its subject matter, and we must pay close attention to the form as well as what the speaker does not (and arguably is unable to) say. As a poem about God, the epitome of holiness, perfection, and wholeness, this poem contains only six lines and is therefore an imperfect, so the reader is confronted with an imperfect rendering of God.

To further unpack the significance of this imperfection, we must understand the biblical importance of the number six, as Spencer's speaker is offering a carefully crafted criticism. I say that this critique is carefully crafted because Spencer does render God through numerical perfection. In her poem "The Wife-Woman," Spencer refers to God as "Maker-of-Sevens" (Greene 186). The number six is a number biblically associated with humanity, and is simultaneously a symbol for humanity and its ills. As

humanity was created on the sixth day and the sixth commandment pro-
hibits the murder of man, the number six is indeed "the number of man"
and denotes human work and imperfection.[20] The number six is also vital
to Christian eschatology, in particular, because of Revelation 13:18, which
reads, "This calls for wisdom. Let the person who has insight calculate the
number of the beast, for it is the number of man. That number is *666*"
(NIV).[21] It is beyond the realm of this analysis to delineate the numerous
interpretations of this verse, but its unequivocal association with being the
antithesis to God and Christianity is germane to this study. That this poem
is metaphorically missing a line sharpens Spencer's critiques because even
before the reader analyzes the diction, the six lines juxtaposed with the
poem's subject matter let the reader know that something is amiss. This
poem becomes a testament to humanity's imperfection but also somewhat
prophetic, as the aforementioned verse calls for an individual "with wisdom" to name and quantify the mark of the beast. The speaker thus assumes
the role of prophet, and the six lines of this poem become a quantification
of the mark of the beast.

The third and fourth lines are rich with a subtle urgency that places a
heft upon the poem and the speaker, and, arguably the essence of the poem
is in these two lines. Though colonization is not explicitly mentioned here,
what the speaker is describing alludes to a history of colonialism, industrialization, and capitalist projects. Her use of "raze" signals not just anni-
hilation but also an abuse of power and denotes that the land has been
brutalized and destroyed, so this poem offers an implicit critique of white
patriarchal supremacist agendas. The speaker proceeds to establish a distinction between what God ordained what humanity has done, and tells us
that "God *never planted*" but instead "*placed a keeper*" (Greene 182; emphasis added). One of the definitions of "plant" is "to colonize or settle," so the
speaker is not just informing us that God did not colonize but also that
colonizing is not a part of his plan for humanity and the natural world.[22]
The speaker's use of "keeper" is also strategic, as it reminds readers that
humankind is tasked with protecting the natural environment, a task that
is akin to the aforementioned "undergardening" described in "Love and
Gardens." Notice that the speaker says the keeper "razed the ground" then
"built a city," suggesting that these acts are sequential and mutually exclusive. The speaker's criticism here has two parts, and she suggests that to
defile nature is tantamount to defiling God. In other words, she claims that
God does not condone the territorializing and corruption of the natural
world for capital or personal gain.

What the speaker does not say is just as important as what she does mention, and her standpoint is central to the poem as well. Once again, we see Spencer's *embodied ecotheology,* as the poem is foregrounded on the implicit presence of Black female bodies. Though she does not explicitly name Blackness and her own Black female body as being central to her anticolonial, anticapitalist critiques, this poem is authored by a Black woman, is spoken by a Black female speaker, and is therefore rendered through Black womanhood. Thus, this poem is also about the razing of Black bodies, especially Black women's bodies, and would not exist without it. One of the hallmarks of Spencer's poetry is that she imagines speakers who are not afraid to articulate themselves on their own terms. I want to take a moment to unpack the complexities of Spencer's Black female speaker because this poem would not work without her. Conscious of her Black womanhood, the speaker demonstrates that she is indeed one with wisdom through the use of deceptively simple poetics and biblical allusions. In true prophet form, she is indeed teaching about the character of God, but she is not didactic; thus, her pedagogy is subtle and carefully crafted. However, the author is also offering a lesson about her divinity and Black women's divinity.

That she does not mention the exploitation of Black bodies, which were stolen and coerced to perform the labor that razed the ground and built the city, underscores the erasure and disappearing from history of Black women's bodies and labor. In other words, the speaker strategically centers her silence and the silence of Black women, forcing the reader to wrestle with their own complicity and either ignore her silence or analyze its complexities. The speaker's silence is emblematic of the invisibilizing of the defilement of Black women's bodies that has been normalized within American consciousness (Williams, "Sin, Nature" 28). The speaker, however, is breaking that silence by visibilizing Black femaleness through her speech. In doing so, she is insisting upon a divineness that has been denied to Black women. Delores Williams explains: "This defilement of nature's body and of black women's bodies is sin, since its occurrence denies that black women and nature are made in the image of God. Its occurrence is an assault upon the spirit of creation in women and nature" (Williams, "Sin, Nature" 29). In this way, the speaker is symbolically addressing the sins of Spencer's "grandsire" and such men who love a dog "because it so perfectly establishes his own human superiority."[23] This poem is certainly a critique of white supremacist colonial and capitalist projects, which the prophet-speaker has the wisdom to name as the mark of the beast. However, this poem can also be read as kind of Black feminist revision to and interpretation of the Genesis creation story, as the speaker highlights that the territorializing and commodification of the natural world and white supremacy are not divinely ordained. In this way, this poem becomes a kind of Black feminist BELT poem because it unites the oppressions of the natural world and Black people through the lens of Black womanhood, and by imagining a God that sees these issues as fundamentally interconnected, it posits a theology that does the same.

Of Spencer's frequently anthologized poem "White Things," Greene makes an observation that beautifully captures the complexities of Spencer's ecotheology: "The white man has tried to dominate nature—both physical objects and human beings. God is nature, and in trying to control nature the white man has endeavored to control God[.] . . . Destruction of the black man is a destruction of God's works, and in doing so the white man with his 'wand of power' had defied God and damned the majority of His creations—'colorful things'" (133–34). That God cannot walk in the city or breathe its air underscores that the city was built upon an imperfect foundation of hatred and exploitation that is not compatible with the image of God. God's inability to be present in the city also gestures toward the environmental damage caused by urbanization and industrialization and points to the depletion of natural resources. Recalling the six lines of the poem and its biblical significance, God's exclusion exposes the city and the ideologies upon which it was built as a kind of antichrist. In this context, "God cannot walk at the eve of day" may also be interpreted as a refusal to entertain humanity's desire to control.

Returning to the opening line of the poem, it may seem somewhat contradictory that Spencer's speaker opens by saying, "God never planted a garden," especially considering her "Love and Gardens" manuscript, which positions God as "The Great Gardener." However, "Love and Gardens" and this poem communicate the same vision of God. In saying that God never planted a garden, she is saying that God never planted a garden *as the keeper did,* so she is insisting upon God's artistry. In doing so, she also insists upon God's mystery and uncontainability and also her own. This poem visibilizes the invisibility of Black women's bodies, positioning them as divine works of art made in God's image. Because God cannot be contained, controlled, and dominated, the speaker also makes the same claim for Black women. The opening lines of the poem become even more urgent and salient when we consider that they are coming from a Black woman. In the same way that she insists upon a God who does not endorse the territorializing of the land, she is also defending herself and insisting upon a God who is against the territorializing of her body. She is insisting upon her right to create a Black woman's God.

Indeed, Spencer draws upon a Christian tradition, but I also want to call attention to how Spencer's use of female speakers and self-affirmation is in line with a gnostic tradition. As Elaine Pagels explains in *The Gnostic Gospels,* gnostic Christians differed from orthodox Christians because they valued self-knowledge, believing that "the psyche bears *within itself* the potential for liberation or destruction" (126; emphasis original). For gnostic Christians, ignorance was tantamount to self-destruction and caused more suffering than sin alone (124). Pagels also notes that for some gnostics, this reliance on self-knowledge extended individuals' conceptions of God: "some gnostic Christians went so far as to claim that humanity created God—and so, from its own inner potential, discovered for itself the revelation of truth" (122). Perhaps what aligns Spencer the most is her use of the female voice—namely, the Black female divine voice. "The Adviser" and "[God never planted a garden]" are evocative of "Thunder, Perfect Mind," a gnostic poem believed to be in the female voice of God or divine feminine power.[24] I want to be clear that Spencer is not merely inverting the image of God through her use of feminine voices. Just as she does with her conception of the natural world; she is re-visioning the image of God and re-visioning spirituality. That Spencer's conception of God may draw upon orthodox Christian and gnostic traditions is consistent with the artistic ingenuity alive in her garden and writing. However, it is imperative to name that this type of spiritual savvy seen in Spencer's work and the work of other Black women writers is one of necessity. In her analysis of *Paradise,* Maha Marouan argues that Morrison's use of gnostic, Candomblé, and Christian traditions "highlights the problematics of an orthodox Christian discourse that does not open up a space for women's spirituality in its full potential, especially as it relates to the moral dichotomies of Christian tradition that reduce women's nature to the virgin or the hag opposition" (100). In other words, while Morrison's use of these religious traditions points to the apertures created through syncretism and hybridity, it also calls attention to the exclusion of Black women's voices and the absence of Black women as spiritual agents. In *Their Eyes Were Watching God,* Janie's grandmother, Nanny, articulates the heft of this exclusion when she shares her desires with Janie: "Ah wanted to preach a great sermon about colored women sittin' on high, but they wasn't no pulpit for me" (15). My reading of Spencer's spirituality affirms Marouan's analysis because I read Spencer's spiritual world-making as a space-making act that amplifies her Black female voice, and this is the same strategy that she utilizes in her poetry. In this way, Spencer is creating a pulpit for herself, so to speak. We can read her God-making as a space-making act in the same vein as the "Chatterton, Shelley, Keats and I—" line in her poem "Dunbar" (Greene 197). In the same way that she writes herself into—and critiques—a literary tradition that excludes Black women, Spencer creates a space—a pulpit—where her theoretical prowess, imagination, and spiritual agency can thrive.

I want to return to the questions that I posed at beginning of this chapter: *What does Spencer's God look like, and what does her God enable her to do?* Spencer's God is a gardener, an adviser, and a being who never planted. Her God looks like whatever she needs and imagines so she can *be*. The texts represented in this chapter are a small fraction of Spencer's archive and writings about God. However, in each text one thing remains: God might be of Spencer and contain her artistic imprint, but his uncontainability, like her own, is constant. Spencer did not believe in or create a God who could be trapped or defined. Rather, God is defined by his indefiniteness and his manyness and his inherent artistry, with his greatest work of art being the natural world. Spencer celebrated the mystery of God, and in her times of need she drew upon her theoretical savviness and creativity and made God accessible to herself. Spencer's writings are testament to the fact that she, too, "found God in herself" and cultivated that divine self-love, a love that enabled her to love herself fiercely. For Spencer, God does not *do;* God *is,* and he enables her to *be* and *become.*

4

"I Proudly Love Being a Negro Woman"

Anne Spencer's "Natural" Means of Expression

James Weldon Johnson was not just a friend to Anne Spencer; he was also her mentor and wanted to see her grow and flourish as a writer. This is perhaps why he sent her a copy of Marguerite Wilkinson's recently published anthology entitled *New Voices: An Introduction to Contemporary Poetry* with a note explaining that this collection of poetry suited her because it "deals with the *newer forms* of poetry, and those are the forms which are your natural means of expression" (qtd. in Greene 56; emphasis original). This gesture was not only a testament to their close friendship, one that would span nearly twenty years, but also it was his acknowledgment of and careful attention to Spencer's aesthetic inclinations. Johnson was able to see something that the critics of her day were unable—or perhaps unwilling—to see.

By aligning Spencer's poetry with these "newer forms," Johnson, as literary critic Jenny Hyest explains, also "located his fellow New Negro writer within another burgeoning literary movement: modernism" (129). It also aligned Spencer with the idea and formation of a "New Poetry," which referred to the broad spectrum of early twentieth-century modernist poetry as we would understand it now. Modernism is central to Spencer's poetry, and Hyest argues that critics have failed to recognize Spencer's modernist aesthetic: "Indeed, Anne Spencer was an important African American poet who helped to forge the emergence of American modernism, though her subsequent erasure from the canon indicates that her modernist aesthetic, which was so apparent to Johnson, has been invisible to the generations of critics succeeding him" (129). As previously noted, critics found Spencer's poetics to be too traditional, apolitical, and raceless. And women in general, with very few exceptions, did not fare very well in critical assessments of literary modernism in the United States. However, it is not that Spencer's modernist poetics are not apparent because her poetics are far from opaque. Rather, Spencer's discursive strategies demand that she and her poetry be understood beyond monolithic visions of Black womanhood and modernism, a task, it seems, that was too complicated for her contemporaries to undertake. Indeed, Spencer summoned Romantic forms and stances, but she did not simply imitate. She summoned to critique. In this chapter, I am interested in Spencer's space-making acts in relation to modernism, and I analyze how she transformed such Romantic forms and stances as sonnets into vehicles for her unapologetically Black feminist voice. "Modernism" is often used as an elusive term to refer to literary productions from the interwar period in the United States. I do not intend to define or redefine it, but, to clarify, I am referring to the literary and cultural movement that took place roughly from the turn of the century and into the early twentieth century. Generally, modernism is characterized by a shift away from tradition; artists emphasized disillusionment, fragmentation, alienation, and discontinuity as they attempted to grapple with modernity. For African American writers, this was the Nadir period/Jim Crow era, so questions of citizenship and representing the African American experience were rendered in their work.

As mentioned in the introduction, one of the limitations of Spencer's archive is the absence of a nuanced account of the inner workings of her literary salon during the New Negro Renaissance. She indeed entertained and corresponded with such intellectuals as W. E. B. Du Bois and Howard Thurman and such fellow New Negro Movement writers as Georgia Douglas Johnson and Langston Hughes in her Virginia home, so her correspondence not only reveals her presence as a New Negro Renaissance artist but demonstrates that, though she was not actively publishing new creative pieces, she was a part of the nexus of artists and thinkers who were imagining new possibilities and potential for Black individuals. Spencer's literary salon and correspondence with prominent figures illustrate her invaluable role as a cultural organizer who was responsible for circulating and fostering New Negro Renaissance ideologies outside of the New York City area, particularly the southern United States.

In this chapter, I continue to locate Spencer within the tradition of Black feminist thought and extend this argument by also associating her formal and aesthetic choices with modernism. This chapter begins by contextualizing Spencer's work within the frame of the New Negro Renaissance and U.S. Black women's modernist poetry.[1] I analyze Spencer's poetry and prose alongside that of her well-known contemporaries and demonstrate how her appropriation of traditional forms reveals a poetics that is both distinctly modern and feminist. Placing her modern discursive strategies in conversation with her contemporaries Nella Larsen, Jessie Redmon Fauset, Alice Dunbar-Nelson, Georgia Douglas Johnson, and Helene Johnson, I argue that Spencer's poetics and discursive choices highlight her identity as a Black woman and, in some cases, are in line with a Black feminist ethos. I situate Spencer with her fellow (and more well-known) New Negro women writers because, as her contemporaries, they, too, faced the challenge of articulating Black women's oppression, and their contributions (both written and cultural) are not consistently recognized. However, it is not my intention to argue that Spencer's exclusion from the canon is unmerited because her work was similar to that of more well-known writers. Instead, I am interested in such formal ingenuity as her daring use of speakers, diction, and traditional poetic forms. When we carefully analyze her use of traditional forms and stances, we see that Spencer is, in fact, "most colored when [she] is thrown against a sharp white background" (Hurston, "How It Feels" 1041).

Furthermore, because one cannot separate her from her garden, I suggest that one of the most modern aspects of Spencer's poetry is the way she deploys her environmental consciousness to both redefine and critique traditional notions of Black womanhood; therefore, just as her feminism necessitated her modernism, so did her environmentalism. It is perhaps her affinity for "newer forms" and the natural world that caused some critics to deem her work unconventional. As a Black woman-poet-mother-wife-civil-rights-and-community-activist-intellectual-librarian-environmentalist, Anne Spencer was an untypical Black woman. She employs this emergent, experimental form of modernism to articulate the breadth of her "untypicalness" and imagines a vision of Black womanhood that is beautifully and audaciously untypical, one that undermines the ideologies espoused in such essays as Elise Johnson McDougald's 1925 essay "The Task of Negro Womanhood."

Writing is an act of making one's self legible, and legibility carries with it the (seemingly logical) assumption of public legibility or the desire to make one's self legible to the public. Spencer, however, was not concerned with public legibility. Spencer's brand of modernism is perhaps best understood in terms of Kevin Quashie's notion of quiet: "Quiet is not a performance or a withholding; instead, it is an expressiveness that is not necessarily legible, at least not in a world that privileges public expressiveness. Neither is quiet about resistance. It is surrender, a giving into, a falling into self. The outer world cannot be avoided or ignored, but one does not only have to yield to its vagaries. One can be quiet" (45). Public legibility was not a priority for Spencer; that she was able to articulate the range of her imagination and humanity in her poetry and prose was enough. Not understanding her is our imaginative deficit as readers, not hers. Anne Spencer was an audaciously untypical woman, and this chapter is ultimately a study of how that "untypicalness" was rendered in her poetry and prose. Themes of fragmentation, alienation, and disorientation are ubiquitous within U.S. literary modernist works, but Spencer's characters and speakers are confident, audacious Black women. Though her critics may have found it difficult to hear a Black woman's voice through her sonnets and iambic pentameter, I would argue that it is precisely because she uses these devices that her voice is clear, resounding, and unapologetically Black. The optics of an assured Black woman articulating herself through mediums associated with white masculinity may seem contradictory, but this is what makes her work and her modernism unique. This was the "natural" means of her expression.

This chapter engages Houston A. Baker Jr.'s *Modernism and the Harlem Renaissance* (1987), James Smethurst's *The African American Roots of Modernism* (2011), and Evie Shockley's *Renegade Poetics* (2011), which have located African American literature within a modernist tradition. Contrary to Baker's argument, I do not intend to argue that Spencer, as a Black artist, did something "different" and aided in the creation of a unique Black modernism. Rather, extending the work of Smethurst's and Shockley's attention to Black artists' formal, thematic, and aesthetic choices, my study of Spencer foregrounds her poetics and formal innovations and aligns her with American modernism. Spencer's frequent interaction and correspondence with fellow New Negro artists position her at the center of the New Negro Renaissance and U.S. literary modernism, more generally. As those of a southern Black woman, Spencer's poetics invite us to think about modernism in the rural South and suggest that a southern Black modernity may not have been concerned entirely with a move toward urbanity and irreconcilable fragmentation.

To understand what distinguishes Spencer's aesthetic decisions as acts of space-making, I need to first situate her within the context of the New Negro Renaissance and of modernism, more generally. "I proudly love being a Negro woman—its [*sic*] so involved and interesting. *We* are the

PROBLEM—the great national game of TABOO" (qtd. in Cullen 47; emphasis original). Anne Spencer penned these words in her epigraph that appears in Countee Cullen's 1927 anthology of Black poets *Caroling Dusk*. Spencer's words, though infused with the sharp wit and sarcasm for which she was known, articulate the varied emotions that many New Negro women writers harbored and highlight the precarious position of Black womanhood during the period. In her use of the word "PROBLEM," Spencer is signaling the popular mind-set that positioned free Blacks as a "problem" and nuisance to the white dominant society from the post-Reconstruction late nineteenth century moving into the twentieth century. Rejection of this ideology and the study of Black disenfranchisement permeated the writings of Black scholars and activists, with W. E. B. Du Bois pioneering research in this area.[2] Invoking the language and ideology of "the Negro problem," Spencer suggests that the Negro problem is also a *gendered* problem and subtly inserts a critique of the multiple oppressions of race, class, gender, and sexuality with which Black women were forced to contend. Spencer's decision to launch this critique in her epigraph is illustrative of the ways in which New Negro women writers appropriated the written word to both express the nuances of their lived experiences and imagine possibilities beyond the realm of their oppression. Gender-biased creative constraints did not prevent New Negro women writers from developing a poetics that granted them the freedom that they were denied in society. New Negro women poets were influenced by nineteenth-century Romantics and Victorians; however, they did not simply replicate the sounds and styles of the traditional forms. Instead, they utilized the forms as tools with which to launch critiques and highlight their positionality as Black women. Such structured forms as sonnets, quatrains, and iambic pentameter were fitting symbols, both visually and metaphorically, for the intersecting oppressions with which Black women had to contend.

Like the nature of the movement itself, New Negro women's discursive strategies are illustrative of a pastiche of styles and influences that reflected their own interests and experiences. However, through their shared desire for Black women's freedom and agency, they employed similar thematic and formal tactics. A discussion of New Negro women's poetics arguably begins with modernism, as the antitraditional, experimentalist qualities of the movement appealed to freedom-seeking women writers. In addition to modernism, Erin D. Chapman argues that the writings of such New Negro women as Jessie Redmond Fauset and Nella Larsen reveal a New Negro women's twentieth-century discourse predicated on four principal themes: racial solidarity, sexual politics, a personal struggle for self-fulfillment, and racial oppression (116). Similarly, Maureen Honey identifies three major themes within New Negro women's poetics: "equation of Blackness and femaleness with strength, resistance to white male oppression, survival of the core self" (*Shadowed Dreams* 18). Formally, New Negro women poets were influenced by such nineteenth-century Romantic poets as Robert Browning and John Keats, in particular, and utilized traditional forms such as sonnets to celebrate Blackness and protest racial oppression. Modernist poets, both Black and white and male and female, appropriated the sonnet form. This was not a phenomenon unique to Black women, but I am interested in the way Black women use the form to articulate their unique standpoint. Black male poets such as Countee Cullen, Sterling Brown, and Claude McKay used the sonnet form, and leading white female modernists such as Edna St. Vincent Millay and Sara Teasdale used it as well.

In *Shadowed Dreams,* Maureen Honey explains that women proudly embraced New Negro ideology that positioned Blacks as self-defined individuals breaking away from stereotypes from the past, and employed various genres to counter the effects of racism and sexism. Honey argues that women viewed their poetry as a means through which to communicate their particular ideas about Blackness and their own individual Black experiences (6–7). New Negro women writers employed these thematic and formal devices to create a safe space beyond the purview of societal mandates in which they could express themselves freely. As Cheryl A. Wall explains, women were able to construct a home through language, one that highlighted their multiple oppressions but did not dwell on it (32). In other words, New Negro women writers *wrote* the freedom they desired and, in doing so, revealed profound meditations on Black womanhood.

As historian Erin D. Chapman explains in *Prove It on Me: New Negroes, Sex, and Popular Culture of the 1920s,* the New Negro Movement ushered in a masculinist focus on racial advancement, one that relegated women to the prescriptive role of race-mothering and shifted Black women's economic and political opportunities during the interwar period (14, 15). This race-mothering ideology is espoused in Elise Johnson McDougald's 1925 essay entitled "The Task of Negro Womanhood":

> Negro women are of a race which is free neither economically, socially, nor spiritually. Like women in general, but more particularly like those of other oppressed minorities, the Negro woman has been forced to

submit to overpowering conditions. Pressure has been exerted upon her, both from without and within her group. Her emotional and sex life is a reflex of her economic station. . . . On the whole the Negro woman's feminist efforts are directed chiefly toward the realization of the equality of the races, the sex struggle assuming the subordinate place. (379, 380–81)

McDougald ends her piece claiming that, in spite of these challenges, Black women are "measuring up to the needs of her family, community and race, and radiating a hope throughout the land" (382). I offer this extended quote to illustrate the structural disadvantages with which Black women had to contend (and still do) coupled with the profound, perpetual self-denial Black women were expected to adopt. McDougald's rhetoric is also illustrative of the rhetoric Black women writers had to undermine. McDougald goes on to argue in her essay that the only militant Black female in history is Sojourner Truth and that Black women are more concerned with racial rather than gender oppression (380–81). This essay appears in Alain Locke's 1925 anthology *The New Negro,* a collection compiled to showcase the accomplishments and possibilities of the New Negro and considered by some critics to be the definitive text of the movement. The irony of this essay is that McDougald, a purported champion of Black women's advancement, inflicts the very gender oppression that Black women sought to combat, and in a collection that was intended to be a public declaration of African Americans' endless potential, Black women are reduced to subservient roles. In spite of such coercive limitations, New Negro women writers created literal and figurative spaces that enabled them to explore the depths of their oppression while theorizing possibilities to facilitate their freedom, happiness, and autonomous sexual and gender expressions.

It is important to situate these women's writings within the broader historical, cultural context of the New Negro Movement and dominant literary trends, more generally, as they serve as both key influences and critical points of departure for New Negro women's writing. Historian Cary D. Wintz argues that the New Negro Movement "was the most important event in twentieth-century African American and cultural life," influencing "every aspect of African American literary and artistic creativity from the end of World War I through the Great Depression" (15). In spite of the New Negro Renaissance being a pivotal African American artistic and cultural movement, women's contributions were largely negated and overlooked prior to the late 1970s through the 1990s Black feminist scholarship of Deborah McDowell, Maureen Honey, Gloria (Akasha) Hull, and Cheryl A. Wall, whose works have recontextualized New Negro Movement women writers and revealed their centrality.[3] As Gloria (Akasha) Hull argues in *Color, Sex, and Poetry:* "Without women writers, the Harlem Renaissance would have been a bleaker place. . . . Poetry, in particular, would have suffered had they not been writing" (30–31).

As with most historical movements and periods, the precise periodization of the New Negro Movement is contested, and its periodization is particularly detrimental to Black women writers. Gloria (Akasha) Hull argues that Black women writers have been "tyrannized by periodization" (30), a sentiment that Cheryl A. Wall echoes in *Women of the Harlem Renaissance,* in which she explains that the periodization of the New Negro Movement has been established largely without the inclusion of women's writings and cultural contributions. This exclusion is why such texts as Zora Neale Hurston's seminal 1937 novel *Their Eyes Were Watching God* are not always considered as a part of the movement (10). In addition to being excluded based on periodization, Gloria (Akasha) Hull and Lorraine E. Roses and Ruth E. Randolph acknowledge that some of Black women's unrecognized work lies in their support networks that existed outside of the limelight. This support includes their sponsorship of cultural components such as the three major literary salons of A'Lelia Walker, Georgia Douglas Johnson, and Anne Spencer in New York (Harlem), Washington, DC, and Lynchburg, Virginia, respectively (Hull 6, 11; Roses and Randolph 2). Regardless of one's preferred periodization, there is no questioning that one of the things that the New Negro Movement did do is connect the social and demographic changes happening to Black people, both men and women, as a result of the Great Migration.

By the 1920s, the New Negro Renaissance had yielded a critical mass of literary and artistic productions. Works such as the first all-Black Broadway production, *Shuffle Along* (1921), and Alain Locke's *The New Negro* (1925) verified that a cultural, artistic renaissance of sorts was taking place. It should be noted that there is no *single* ideology that unifies the New Negro Movement; its quality is "ephemeral" in nature and resists cohesive classification (Wintz 15). However, the New Negro Movement was both influenced by and arguably a fulcrum for U.S. literary modernism, which had become the dominant artistic expression, philosophical movement, and cultural trend of the early twentieth century. Making its American literary and cultural debut approximately at the turn of the century, modernism was a highly critical, disillusioned philosophical approach, one that departed from traditional thinking (i.e., Enlightenment ideology), questioned bourgeois thought, and articulated a sense of fragmentation and alienation both from one's self and society in a newly urbanized, industrial society. These themes characterize the fiction of such canonical (white) American writers as Ernest Hemingway, F. Scott Fitzgerald, William Faulkner, Gertrude Stein, and Robert Frost, whose writings are seen as emblematic of the movement.

In *Modernism and the Harlem Renaissance,* Houston A. Baker Jr. addresses the alienation and exclusion of Black authors and texts from conversations about modernism and argues that it is not exclusively a white Western phenomenon. Baker argues that African Americans did have and created a distinct form of modernism, one that is identifiable in New Negro Renaissance writing, and he argues that this period "included some of the earliest attempts by Afro-American artists and intellectuals to define themselves in 'modern' terms" (9). For Baker, Afro-American modernism was a separate entity, which he terms "modern Afro-American sound," grounded in southern culture and "a function of a specifically Afro-American discursive practice" (xiv), one that was a conscious rejection of "bourgeois formalisms" and moves away from the tropes associated with slavery (101). Baker aptly locates such writers as Sterling Brown, Charles Chesnutt, Ralph Ellison, and Jean Toomer within the Afro-modernist tradition; however, noticeably absent from Baker's analysis is a discussion of New Negro women's contributions and modernist aesthetic.

In *Portraits of the New Negro Woman,* Cherene Sherrard-Johnson implicitly engages Baker's masculinist focus and centers her analysis on the ways in which African American women writers and visual artists deployed characteristics of Afro-modernism during the New Negro Movement. As previously noted, a favorite tactic of New Negro women writers was that of appropriating and revising traditional forms and themes. One trope that was of particular importance to New Negro women was the mulatta figure, whose "tragic mulatta narratives" were popularized in the nineteenth century by writers like Lydia Maria Childs. Sherrard-Johnson argues that during the New Negro Movement, both visual and literary artists became "obsessed" with mulatta iconography (xix). The mulatta figure became the symbol of an idealized Black womanhood, one that was unattainable for most, functioning "as an ambiguous symbol of racial uplift that ironically constrained African American womanhood in the early twentieth century" (xx). Like Baker, Sherrard-Johnson concurs that a distinct Afro-modernism existed during the New Negro Movement, one that is characterized by irony, masking, and parody (52). She identifies New Negro women writers' appropriation of the mulatta figure as evidence of such traits because these writers complicated the mulatta figure by having their female protagonists articulate feminist and modernist perspectives; because of New Negro women's revisions, the New Negro Movement also witnessed the ascendancy of a "new mulatta" (105).

Such revisions to the mulatta trope can be seen in Nella Larsen's *Passing* (1929) and Jessie Redmond Fauset's *Plum Bun* (1929), both of whose authors reimagine their mulatta protagonists and depart from old tropes of tragedy. For writers like Fauset and Larsen who drew upon the tragic mulatta figure, she served as "a narrative device of mediation" and site of alternative imagination as well (qtd. in Sherrard-Johnson xix). Writers could transform the safe, idealized iconography of the mulatta and use her as a tool to address the conflicting issues of racial solidarity, sexual and gender inequality, the desire for self-fulfillment, and racial oppression with which Black women were forced to contend on a daily basis. Sherrard-Johnson argues, "The mulatta as icon, then, became a representative of unspeakable subjugation and erotic desire, both inter- and intraracial. Styled as the ideal template for measuring black femininity, she was, by turns, a constrained symbol of Victorian womanhood, a seductive temptress, and a deceptive, independent, modern woman" (xix). Hence, Larsen's and Fauset's modernist revisions to the tragic mulatta, Künstlerromans, and marriage plots enable them to both imagine Black womanhood with freedom and sexual autonomy and articulate Black feminist concerns.

Nearly thirty years before Fauset's and Larsen's revisions to the tragic mulatta trope, Spencer provided her own critique. Though she is primarily known as a poet, Spencer's first publication was a short story titled "Beth's Triumph" and published in 1900 in the *Colored American Magazine* under her maiden name, Anne Bethel Scales. This publication also provides insight into the origins of her chosen pen name. Spencer's birth name is "Annie Bethel Scales." Her birth name is also sometimes listed cited as "Annie Bethel Scales Bannister" (Greene 4). James Weldon Johnson is credited for suggesting she use "Anne" as her pen name, writing, "I have decided that Anne Spencer is the way in which you should sign—that makes a splendid pen name" (qtd. in Greene 53). Johnson made this suggestion in 1921, but it is important to note that she published her first story using "Anne" nearly twenty years before this suggestion was made (Greene 49, 53). Perhaps this is why she responded, "I like the pen name—really I like everything that belongs to me!'" (qtd. in Greene 53).

This short story revolves around the refusal of a marriage proposal and tells the stories of Beth and Louise, two young women approaching graduation. Beth serves as the narrator and provides a nuanced account of Louise's dilemma: Louise receives a coercive marriage proposal from a Mr. Warwick, whom she does not want to marry because she is in love with a man named Tom, but she feels as though she is left with no other choice. The story is set in the spring of 1899, so, as Louise is a young Black woman, her freedom to choose is indeed constrained. Louise appeals to Beth for assistance, and Beth serendipitously has a clairvoyant dream that exposes Mr. Warwick as a fraud, forcing him to leave town, thus freeing Louise from an obligatory marriage. The story is fantastical in nature with a gesture toward speculative or gothic fiction. Its unrealistic ending only highlights the degree to which a Black woman "knows little of peace and happiness" (McDougald 382). What is remarkable about this story is that it is Beth's dream that literally sets Louise free. More specifically, it is Beth's *audacity* to share her dream that sets Louise free. This dream is illustrative of the kind of creative, unencumbered individual self-fashioning that she and Louise lack as Black women at the turn of the century, but Spencer imagines a character so bold and so daring as to be herself. To be an audacious Black woman in the twenty-first century is dangerous; Spencer was daring enough to imagine this in 1900. In Spencer's Black women's world, being an audacious Black woman is not dangerous, but Beth is undaunted and articulates herself confidently and effortlessly.

This ability to dream is also of significance to Beth and Louise because their narratives could easily be reduced to a formulaic mulatta trope. Early in the story, Beth signals both her own and Louise's mixed-race ancestry:

> Louise was no baby; but a tall, beautiful, strong-minded girl, with two soft peach-blooms upon her cheeks, and a complexion like the rich Jersey cream; hair probably not so nice or beautiful as that of some of *our other girls*—mine for example, but it invariably looked *better. . .* According to the latest mirror census, I have a shock of thick red-brown hair, which my friends please me by calling auburn; a nondescript complexion, a face that might pass, were it not for the bane of my life—its nose. (Scales, pt. 1, 153; emphasis added)

Beth does not mention her or Louise's racial background again, so her careful descriptions at the story's beginning may seem incidental. However, Spencer's treatment of Beth's and Louise's mixed ancestry is intimately connected to Beth's dream. Beth's dream does not only represent a desire for greater agency and the ability to fashion one's gender identity and destiny; it also represents a desire for a new narrative. Indeed, like her successors, Spencer deliberately utilizes mulatta iconography as a "narrative device of mediation" (qtd. in Sherrard-Johnson xix). Spencer includes these details about Beth's and Louise's fair complexions because she knows they will signify something in the reader's consciousness, and by not making their ancestry essential to the narrative, she provides a critique of the formulaic tragic mulatta trope and simultaneously extends an invitation for other Black women writers to dream along with her. As the title suggests, this story is also about Beth, and what is triumphant about her narrative is that she, herself, is not a tragic mulatta, and she has the audacity to imagine a Black woman's world in which such a trope does not exist. She can simply be and dream freely. In this way, Beth's dream creates an aperture through which such characters as Angela Murray, Clare Kendry, and Irene Redfield can be imagined. Beth's dream is a powerful declaration that illustrates that Black women's freedom is possible if they are allowed to dream and articulate themselves.

This story is probably a creative rendering of incidents from Spencer's personal life prior to her marriage to Edward. Spencer's mother, Sarah, wanted to ensure that her daughter married "well"; therefore, Spencer was subjected to entertaining Sarah's prospects for her. One such individual was principal at a nearby school whom Spencer nicknamed "the Walrus," and another individual, Dr. Holley, had two children and was married, though he was pursuing a divorce from his wife who was in an asylum (Greene 41). Spencer had already decided to marry Edward, and one evening, in an attempt to escape an evening visit from "the Walrus," Spencer jumped from her window and sprained both of her ankles, a daring leap from which she claimed that she never quite recovered (Greene 42).[4] Spencer's revision to the tragic mulatta trope could also possibly reflect her own disdain for skin color hierarchy and colorism. In his biography of Spencer, J. Lee Greene writes that Spencer recalled her mother's skin color prejudice, and Greene theorized that perhaps her mother's disapproval of her marriage to Edward was due to his darker skin (42–43). I offer these anecdotes to reiterate that, for Spencer, the personal was political and to highlight what Greene concluded about Spencer's willful nature: "As a young adult she exercised an independence of mind that was to be characteristic of her entire life" (42). Spencer's feminism was audacious and daring, both in her writing and personal life, and she fervently believed in a woman's right to individuality.

Her rootedness and strong sense of self enabled her to reimagine Black womanhood, in fiction and in her daily life. The undaunted, uncompromised voice of a Black woman is what makes her work uniquely modern. Spencer's work stands out because she presents us with representations of whole, steadfast Black female subjects and speakers during an era fraught with themes of self-alienation and disassociation.

In *Black Women Poets of the Harlem Renaissance,* Emmanuel Egar establishes a binary distinction between New Negro men and women writers and argues that women's poetry is unlike men's poetry in that it is not "war song" (ix). Using Claude McKay's poem "If We Must Die" as the quintessential masculine poetic "war song," Egar argues that New Negro women poets were more interested in poetry for poetry's sake, and their poetics lack the unbridled emotion and protest of that of their male counterparts (ix). Cheryl A. Wall concedes that women were indeed bound by traditional forms such as marriage plots, and speculates that this creative constraint prevented Jessie Redmon Fauset from writing more novels (83). However, Maureen Honey identifies the restraint and gentility seen in some New Negro women's poetry as an act of self-protection, "an acknowledgment that the forces arrayed against a Black woman's dignity and development of her powers are formidable" (*Shadowed Dreams* 17). Nonetheless, she vehemently cautions against dismissing women's poetry as being apolitical and failing to address issues of race, gender, sexuality, and oppression (17).

This theme of self-protection is found in New Negro women's poetics, and it is one that signals to the tradition of masking in African American literature. Masking is far more complex than a rhetorical strategy or literary subterfuge; it was a necessary component of virtually all forms of African American expression, New Negro women writers included. Through the act of metaphorically and literally codifying their work, artists were able to express themselves freely and negotiated spaces for Black expression, and most importantly, beyond the comprehension and reproach of dominant society. This "self-veiling" strategy New Negro women adopted in their poetics has roots in masking and therefore positions New Negro women writers, not as genteel, apolitical writers but as actors continuing a longstanding tradition (18).

Alice Dunbar-Nelson's "I Sit and Sew" (1927) and Georgia Douglas Johnson's "The Heart of a Woman" (1918) are emblematic of this type of self-veiling, as they explore the issue of unspeakable, sequestered female desire. Like the meticulous stitching the speaker of the poem bemoans, the form of Dunbar-Nelson's poem is neatly constrained within four stanzas of rhyming couplets in iambic pentameter. The speaker's final cry in the last line of the poem indicates that her agitation has increased, and she addresses God: "It stifles me—God, must I sit and sew?" (21). These final lines are both a plea for divine intervention and a fervent reminder that she is capable of more than just monotonous sewing. We get a sense that the speaker is not only alienated from the world around her but also alienated from herself, as she is unable either to realize her desires or even to speak them. One of the curious aspects of this poem is that it remains provocatively unclear what the speaker desires. The theme of unutterable desire also raises questions about sexuality, namely lesbianism, as scholars have speculated that Dunbar-Nelson's sexuality was fluid, and she may have been bisexual (Hull 24). The poem is both a cry for the speaker to have the opportunity and freedom for self-expression and a thorough critique of the lack of freedom available to Black women. Like all Black women, the speaker is confined and unfree. This recurring motif of confinement is endemic to the African American literary tradition and is arguably an intentional poetic choice, as it was the fitting metaphor to describe Black women's challenges both creatively and existentially.

Georgia Douglas Johnson's poem "The Heart of a Woman" continues this metaphor of confinement and likens a woman's latent desires to being locked in an "alien cage" breaking "on the sheltering bars" (5, 8). Johnson's poem is highly allusive, evoking Paul Laurence Dunbar's well-known poem "Sympathy" (1893). Dunbar assigns his bird a male gender, writing, "I know why the caged bird beats *his* wing" (5; emphasis added). We can interpret Johnson's poem as a Black feminist response and revision to Dunbar's poem, underscoring that this yearning for freedom and refusal to accept bondage is a sentiment that Black women feel in both their creative and personal lives.

Though Egar contends that New Negro women's poetics lacked the fervor of their male counterparts, they penned highly political protest pieces. Helene Johnson's "Sonnet to a Negro in Harlem" (1927) is one such example, and like her aforementioned contemporaries, Johnson appropriates a traditional form. Johnson writes her poem in sonnet form to articulate her feelings of love, not for a specific individual or lover, but rather in a more generalized, gender-neutral fashion to articulate her love for Blackness in all forms. In its celebration of the beauty of the Black body, the rhetoric of the poem anticipates the "Black Is Beautiful" mantra that stemmed from the Black Power Movement of the 1960s and 1970s:

You are disdainful and magnificent—
Your perfect body and your pompous gait,
Your dark eyes flashing solemnly with hate
Small wonder that you are incompetent

. . . .

I love your laughter arrogant and bold.
You are too splendid for this city street! (1–4, 13–14)

The juxtaposition of "perfect body" and "pompous gait" invokes the ways in which pseudoscience used the Black body in a way that deemed it inferior, and the speaker in the poem is affirming that there is nothing wrong with the Black body; it is perfect as it stands. The use of "hate" in the subsequent line is a term that could incite fear, as emotions in excess are feared when expressed by the Black body. Here, the use of "hate" refers to an unjust and unequal society, and "solemnly with hate" is meant to denote sincere thought and consideration. This "hate" is rooted in injustice, and it is Johnson's way to signal the wish for the feelings of hate to be something other than what they are. It also signals that these feelings are serious; they are not merely emotional, visceral, or reactionary. There is also a class element because, after all, this is a young working-class Black woman on the corner, not a "respectable" middle-class man. The words "small wonder" playfully evoke stereotypes of Black incompetence, as this type of language was typically used to demean Black people and question their aptitude. However, the suggestion here is that this "incompetence" is not what the dominant society would make it out to be. Rather, the "incompetence" refers to the New Negro's inability to imitate a society that rejects *this* New Negro; in this usage, the word implies that anyone who has their own sense of self and confidence has no desire to imitate others. In her use of a sonnet, Johnson herself is critiquing imitation as she herself imitates, but both her poem and depiction of the New Negro are a testament to the fact that the New Negro does not want to merely imitate.

The poem ends with the speaker looking at the Negro in Harlem and appreciating their acceptance of self-worth. This is a powerful protest poem that gives an image of the excessively high capability of the New Negro, and Johnson illustrates that this excessiveness has to occur, and the speaker must affirm them because the Negro is in an environment that will not affirm them. Ultimately this is a declaration that the "Negro in Harlem" cannot be contained and that their greatness exceeds the environment that seeks to contain them. Despite critics like Egar who contend that New Negro women's poetics falls short of a "war cry," Johnson's sonnet is thematically similar to McKay's proclamation in "If We Must Die," which is also written in sonnet form. The lines "In vain; then even the monsters we defy/Shall be constrained to honor us though dead!" is ultimately both a rejection of racism and a declaration of the New Negro (273).

Like her aforementioned contemporaries, Spencer also appropriated traditional forms. Spencer's admiration for the Romantics and Victorians is clearly seen in her poetry, and she was particularly fond of Robert Browning, for whom her poem "Life Long, Poor Browning" is written. Poet and literary critic Holly Karapetkova cautions against the hasty dismissal of Spencer's work and argues that Spencer's use of traditional Romantic forms reveals that her poetic choices were "profoundly, modern, black, and female" (229).[5] Like Browning, Spencer penned dramatic monologue poems that include "Change," "Lines to a Nasturtium (A Lover Muses)," and, arguably her most well-known dramatic monologue poem, "Before the Feast at Shushan" (Karapetkova 230). Similar in style and tone to Browning's "My Last Duchess," "Before the Feast at Shushan," Karapetkova argues, reveals the poetics of a Black, modern woman concerned with gender and racial oppression: "The poem is, ultimately, about [Vashti's] desire to be treated equally as a human being, regardless of her gender" (Karapetkova 233). Thus, Spencer utilizes the form of a dramatic monologue to explore the relationship between gender, race, and power, which, Jenny Hyest argues, is the crux of Spencer's feminist modernist poetics: "Spencer sought to represent women's lived experience of oppression by exploring the psychodynamics of male dominance and female resistance" (130). In addition to the dramatic monologue poem, Spencer also utilizes a dialogue form (in "The Lemming: O Sweden") and the portrait poem (in "Lady, Lady" and "At the Carnival") (Karapetkova 234, 238). In each of these instances Spencer's voice, the voice of a Black woman, is audible; Spencer utilizes the form to question the "exclusive whiteness and maleness that dominated modernist [and Romantic] writing" (240).

Scholars have identified a feminist poetics in Spencer's writing, a not uncommon linkage in modernist poetry by U.S. women writers, especially those who stayed in the United States. Early bohemia in the United States was a feminist place. Jenny Hyest contends that a symbiotic relationship existed between Spencer's feminist politics and experimental style: "Spencer's feminism necessitated her modernism. Her desire to break with established social formations demanded the development of modernist poetic practices. At a moment when many white male modernists were conceiving of themselves as participating in a literary phenomenon that excluded women and resisted feminist movements, Spencer was producing poetry that directly linked the revolutions of literary modernism with equally radical transformations in gender politics" (131). Though scholars have regarded Spencer's poetry as traditional, her poetics are inextricably linked to her lived experience as a Black woman, and she was acutely aware of the nuances of her positionality as a working-class Black woman. In his 1977 biography of Spencer, J. Lee Greene laments, "Her failure to write primarily or unmistakably about being black in America is perhaps one reason her works have not received the attention they deserve" (129). However, Greene concedes that she was equally concerned with both "the race question" and "the woman question" (128). Evie Shockley cautions against the hasty dismissal of Spencer's poetry as raceless, noting that such labeling is gender-biased and suggests that a Black aesthetic cannot also be feminist: "To point toward womanhood is too commonly equated with pointing away from blackness. Such gendered misconceptions would necessarily render Spencer's black aesthetics invisible, insofar as her poetic engagement with the concerns that preoccupied 'the New Negro' frequently emerges from or focuses on issues and situations involving women's lives or women's equality" (132–33).

We can see Spencer's feminist modernist poetics at work in her portrait poem "At the Carnival" (1922), which must be understood not only in terms of modernist experimentation but also Black womanhood (and perhaps satire and sarcasm as well). The speaker does not use high poetic language in this poem, but she utilizes pseudoclassical, pseudo-epic name taglines such as "Girl-of-the-Diving-Tank" (Greene 176). There is also a way in which we can see this poem in conversation with Georgia Douglas Johnson's "The Heart of a Woman" because the older woman in "At the Carnival" arguably wishes the young women a hasty death to spare her from the tragedy that is Black womanhood, which is the very tragedy the speaker in Johnson's poem laments. The element of being on display is key to this poem, and that the woman wishes death upon the young girl after she becomes aware of both her own and the crowd's gaze and her own linkage and identification with the girl so that the girl embodies the speaker's early possibilities and the speaker the girl's fate—much like "The Heart of a Woman." There is a rising and falling action of this poem in which the older woman "desires a name" for the young girl only to conclude with a death-wish (Greene 176). In the recognition of her own gaze, the older woman also recognizes the futility in naming the young girl, as naming her would not change her fate; she realizes her inability to effect change:

Little Diver, Destiny for you,
Like as for me, is shod in silence;
Years may seep into your soul
The bacilli of the usual and the expedient;
I implore Neptune to claim his child to-day! (Greene 177)

Address and diction are key to this poem and give it the quality of a Greek tragedy. In her dramatic monologue, the speaker addresses the young diver, the audience/reader, and finally Neptune, so even though this poem is literally narrating what is taking place "at the carnival," the speaker shifts her attention to speaking more generally about the young girl's future outside of the carnival. The poem then shifts from becoming a contained dramatic monologue to a prologue to a Greek tragedy with the "Gay little Girl-of-the-Diving-Tank" positioned as our hero whose narrative ends in death. If we juxtapose Johnson's and Douglas's poems, there is a way in which the older woman's desire for the young girl's death is a kind of mercy killing, one that spares her from the inevitability of performing the prescriptive Black womanhood seen in Douglas's poem. The extreme sorrow in this Greek tragedy is Black womanhood. This poem is a beautiful example of Spencer's untypicalness because she imagines Black women's oppression through the lens of a Greek tragedy and creates a speaker daring enough to say that a swift death is better than a life "shod in silence" (Greene 177). This poem launches a severe critique by ultimately suggesting that it is better not to bring little Black children into the world, a sentiment that mirrors W. E. B. Du Bois's own sentiments in *The Souls of Black Folk* in the essay "Of the Passing of the First-Born" about his young son's death (353). That Spencer juxtaposes this scathing criticism with the banality of a carnival functions as a critique that highlights prescriptive notions of New Negro womanhood, notions that Spencer herself eschewed. In other words, even at a carnival, Black women are "struck in the face daily by contempt" (McDougald 382).

Spencer's invoking a classical style also gives this poem a self-referential quality. She is invoking a tradition that is not associated with articulating Black womanhood, so the pairing seems incongruent.[6] In doing so, Spencer is signaling the ways in which she is aware of how literary canons have the ability to silence her voice as a Black woman. Karapetkova explains:

But what shines through in Spencer's poem is not an elusive or distant glimpse of a woman as a work of art, as in many modernist portraits, but a specific and singular relationship between the speaker and the diver, two women artists. . . . Indeed, the fact that Spencer herself and other women of the Harlem Renaissance managed to survive as artists and to leave us such works of beauty provides for many contemporary readers the type of surprise and awakening that the diver-artist provides for the speaker of the poem. (Karapetkova 240)

The poem itself is a testament to the fact that Spencer will not be silenced, and by creating a speaker who is bold and undaunted, there is a way in which one can read this poem as Spencer's staking a claim for Black women writers, and that is certainly valid. However, Spencer is doing precisely what Greene and her critics claim she failed to do clearly: articulating her lived experience as a Black woman. She simply did it in her terms.

To further unpack Spencer's modern poetics, we must analyze her strategic use of other traditional poetic forms. The undated, posthumously published poem "For E.A.S." (which are her husband's initials) appears to be quintessentially traditional, as it is written in the form of an Italian/ Petrarchan sonnet in iambic pentameter, ends with a Shakespearean couplet, and the topic of love is its central theme.[7] The poem opens with the speaker recalling statements made to her that seem to lament the obligatory confines and gender inequalities of matrimony:

This, then, entire, is what they say to me—
Demeanor peeved and fretted brow the while:
"So bad the man you sleep beside is free;
In lonely sadness must you go your mile: (Greene 184)

To this the speaker responds:

The pity that *they* should be such fools
As think weak traps may hold a fragrant breath;
That clumsy note played poorly still by rules
Can fill a life with living grace till death. . . .
Himself, the song my silly notes enjoy
His, too, the star I see, the dream employ. (Greene 184;
    emphasis original)

Thematically, this poem implicitly engages Johnson's and Dunbar-Nelson's poems, and we can think of the second stanza as a revision or response to their poems. In the first stanza, the speaker echoes the sentiments of Alice Dunbar-Nelson's and Georgia Douglas Johnson's above poems, and Black womanhood is characterized as a state of restricted "lonely sadness," whereas Black men are "free." In the second stanza, the tone of the poem shifts, and the speaker responds to the "fools" by explaining that her marriage is loving and egalitarian. In the final couplet, she likens her relationship to a "song" and a "star," which carry connotations of unfettered possibility. This connotation underscores that, for her, matrimony is not a space of monotonous unspeakable desire. Instead, she offers a vision of womanhood and marriage in which individuality not only coexists but also thrives.

Indeed, Spencer is offering a feminist critique of normative gender roles in matrimony, but the formal devices and her speaker enable her to destabilize the exclusionary nature of the canon. The poem's form and structure appear mundanely traditional, but we must remember that this Black female speaker is speaking from her perspective as a Black woman. When we juxtapose the form and the poem's content, what the speaker is saying is quite daring. Spencer is writing about Black womanhood and Black love using forms associated with a white, male literary canon. She is not simply replicating traditional sounds, styles, and forms; she is appropriating them, and, in doing so, she is making herself, as a Black woman, legible. The brilliance of this poem lies in the fact that a Black woman's voice is heard clearly through traditionally white, masculine forms. Spencer's ingenuity is almost deceptive and evokes the African American literary tradition of masking because the poem's structure carries significations with particular aforementioned expectations and associations.[8] She changes the terms of signification, and the reader must accept her terms in order to understand her. This subtle move is profoundly daring, not just because she is literally shifting the canon for herself but also because she is setting forth the terms upon which she is to be understood.

That Spencer chose these forms through which to articulate Black womanhood speaks to untypicalness and audaciousness and the degree to which she was able to imagine a Black woman's world. This audacious move of destabilizing the canon and making room for herself is something that Spencer began her career doing. In her 1920 poem entitled "Dunbar," named after Paul Laurence Dunbar), she boldly inserts herself into the canon: "Chatterton, Shelley, Keats and I—/Ah, how poets sing and die!" (Greene 197).[9] Spencer includes herself alongside major English Romantic poets, implicitly and explicitly claiming that they are equals. Spencer invites readers to partake in her imaginative prowess and ability to conceive of a Black woman's world free from such hierarchies.

I want to revisit Spencer's critical environmental consciousness and consider it through the lens of modernism. As discussed in chapter 2, Spencer maps the experiences of Black womanhood onto the natural world. Spencer's concern with her right to self-fashioned humanity is seen through her use of natural world symbols, and it is perhaps this affinity for modernism and the natural world that caused some critics to deem her work "too unconventional" (qtd. in Greene 56). This creative move of fusing a Black feminist politics and environmentalism is not only modern but also *daring*. Spencer's modernism is revealed and arguably best understood when we juxtapose her gender politics and her environmental consciousness. Spencer's invoking of her garden indeed reveals her Romantic influence, but it is also illustrative of the way in which New Negro women utilized natural world symbolism.

Though ecoliterary criticism remains an overlooked site of inquiry in Black women's writing, Maureen Honey addressed the significance of the natural world to New Negro women writers more than thirty years ago in *Shadowed Dreams* (1989). Honey argues that such women writers as Spencer, Zora Neale Hurston, Bessie Mayle, Ethel Lee Newsome, and Mae Cowdery identified with nature because it was something that, like them, had been corrupted and dominated by white male oppression; therefore, they used nature as a vehicle through which they could articulate their gender and racial oppression (8). Their use of natural images can be read as a form of resistance through which they may assert their sexual autonomy in the world and imagine greater freedom. Since what is natural is used to mobilize what is normative, their use of natural world symbols signals their attempt to destabilize normativities and assert their right to define their sexualities as they choose. Evie Shockley also rejects the gender-biased (mis) labeling of Spencer's and New Negro Renaissance women writers' poetry as conventionally feminine because of their use of natural world imagery:

> When we talk or write about "nature" in the context of the U.S., race, gender, and class issues are deeply implicated. The focus in Spencer's poetry on gardens has been alternately dismissed and defended on the grounds of gender, as critics either condescendingly excused New Negro Renaissance women poets for choosing "genteel" subjects or pointed out the ways appearing to conform to feminine norms could accommodate "coded" treatment of purportedly masculine topics. At

the same time, her poetry foregrounding flora and fauna has been characterized as "raceless," a discourse that supports the equation between
black nationalism and the black male figure, on the one hand, and the
one between African American experience and urban life that begins
around World War I and becomes increasingly prevalent over the
twentieth century. (145)

Spencer's garden served as a powerful symbol within both her writing and
personal life, and Shockley argues that the centrality of Spencer's garden
invites an alternative reading of the New Negro Renaissance because her
work "challenges us to further reconsider constructions of the New Negro
Renaissance, recalling that Afro-modernity in the South was not predicated upon a wholesale removal from the natural world to an urban industrial one, but was signaled instead, perhaps by the precious acquisition of a
garden of one's own" (144).

The poem "Lines to a Nasturtium (A Lover Muses)" (1926) is a stunning
example of Spencer's modernism, feminism, and environmental consciousness. The poem is a celebration of a lover's beauty and desire for her, but the
final five lines are arguably the most provocative because they are rife with
Spencer's unfettered imagination:

> Hands like, how like, brown lilies sweet,
> Cloth of gold were fair enough to touch her feet . . .
> Ah, how the sense reels at my repeating,
> *As once in her fire-lit heart I felt the furies*
> Beating, beating. (Greene 185; emphasis original)

Indeed, this is a love poem, "a lover's apostrophe to a flower," that, like
Spencer's above poem, appears rife with thematic conventionality, as the
object of desire is female and likened to flora (Shockley 130). However,
Spencer's speaker and diction defy the expectations of these conventions
and provide a beautiful rupture in normativity. Take, for example, the use
of "brown lilies" and the speaker's unidentified gender. The speaker likens
their lover's hands to "brown lilies sweet," so is signaling that their object
of desire is probably a Black woman. I intentionally use the gender-neutral
pronoun "they" (and its variations) to reinforce my reading of the speaker's
unidentified gender. I shift to using "she" later in my analysis because I will
argue that this speaker could likely be female. This move of locating their
Black female lover's beauty within the natural world is both dangerous and
expansive. It is dangerous because it conjures ideologies of dominion and

references colonial legacies that rendered Black women's bodies as a kind of natural resource to be exploited in terms of labor, sex, and reproduction (all of which are practically and syntactically related). There is an expansiveness here as well because Spencer has boldly reimagined a Black woman's beauty and desirability through the lens of the natural world. "Brown lilies" is also a stunning linguistic subtlety because Spencer is playing with (and undermines) the well-known colloquialism of "lily white"/"lily whiteness" as a figuration of idealized beauty and purity.

Though scholars have read the speaker of this poem as a male persona, Spencer is imagining a world in in which conventions are not followed, so the speaker does not have to be male. As in the work of Angelina Weld Grimké, lesbian poets used the tradition of women writing poems in a man's voice to allow them to write love poems to women in a time when homosexuality was against the law and openly gay literature was deemed pornography in the United States. The speaker's race is also unidentified, but since Spencer is a Black woman, it is reasonable (and arguably logical) to assume that her speakers are also Black women. Evie Shockley also discusses the speaker's unidentified race and gender and suggests the possibility that the speaker could be a white male, contextualizing her analysis within the context of post- Reconstruction respectability politics and anti-Black violence (132–33). Since Spencer has created a world in which a Black woman's beauty is revered through the chocolate hues of brown lilies, entertaining the possibility of a female speaker is in line with her undaunted imagination. The provocative ambiguity surrounding the speaker's gender is a queer gesture on Spencer's part, and with the possibility of a female speaker, this poem becomes a beautiful celebration of queer love and desire, as it is rich with highly erotic, sexual language. "Queer" is a notoriously slippery word, and I want to be very careful to note that I am not suggesting that Spencer herself was queer. I simply want to call attention to the way she makes this poem available to a queer reading. In my use of "queer," I draw from Cathy Cohen's expansive, yet critical, definition of "queer" that includes individuals outside of heteronormative frames of power (452–62).

In the final three lines, the speaker becomes so consumed with thoughts of her lover (and intimacy with her lover) that she loses herself in time and space. That the speaker is unidentified is provocative (and also daring), not just because of its queer implications but also because we must recall that Spencer equips her speakers with the audaciousness to articulate themselves. This speaker is no exception, so their ambiguity *is* audacious. What is ambiguous to the reader is a clear articulation from the speaker. This ambiguity raises the question of public legibility. As with Spencer's body of "unconventional" poetry, the failure to understand or accept the speaker on their terms is our deficit, as readers, not the speaker's. What on the surface appears to be conventional, female poetry is actually a poem that moves away from normativities.

Spencer was an audacious, untypical Black woman, and her writings are infused with her steadfast sense of self. Spencer's modernism is seen in the way she is undaunted in articulating and being herself. This is evident in the ways she imagines speakers who are not afraid to articulate themselves and utilizes traditional forms associated with white masculinity to articulate Black femaleness. What is modern about Spencer's poetry is that she was solely concerned with expressing her beingness and humanity by any means necessary—even if it were gender queer persona or through traditional formal devices. What is consistent throughout Spencer's poetry is that her voice and her untypicalness are always clear and uncompromised.

Though James Weldon Johnson linked her to modernism, this is a designation that Spencer likely would have rejected. In an undated entry entitled "Modern Poetry," Spencer shares her opinions on such "newer forms": "The newness of this or any subject presented with a certain timing, can lose its patina and grow old at the stroke of midnight if we must depend too much on . . . as we say 'what's new'? Objective poetry grows old before subjective poetry does because refrigerators must be kept to date but the heart within us changes only for convenience."[10] Thus, if Spencer's poetry reveals modernistic inclinations, her statement suggests that her aesthetic and formal choices were made independent of any trends. Her audacious authenticity was the *natural* means of her expression.

5

Do Not Separate Them from Their Gardens

Black Women's Writings and Ecopoetics

> My first step from the old white man was trees. Then air. Then birds.
> Then other people.... Whenever you trying to pray, and man plop
> himself on the other end of it, tell him to git lost, say Shug. Conjure up
> flowers, wind, water, a big rock.
>
> —Shug Avery, in *The Color Purple,* by Alice Walker

This project is an attempt to not separate Spencer from her garden but to also remind us to not separate Black women from themselves and their writings of the natural world, so it is only fitting to end with a study of Black women writers to whom we need to listen. This concluding chapter examines the ecopoetics of other Black women writers and reveals the rich meditations on Black womanhood that are available when Black women writers are not separated from themselves. Scenes from Zora Neale Hurston's *Their Eyes Were Watching God,* Alice Walker's *The Color Purple,* and Dionne Brand's *In Another Place, Not Here* illustrate the rich legacy of Black women's natural world writings and underscore how readings of Black women's literature may be enhanced when we consider their ecological materialities. So, what I offer here is an invitation to bear witness to Black women's ecological materialities. And keeping a Spencerian logic in mind, we should also ask, *What is revealed when we do not separate Black women from their gardens?*

Janie's pear tree, Maud Martha's daffodils, and Shug Avery's transformation of God from male authoritarian into trees, birds, and air represent a rich, yet overlooked, tradition of Black women's natural world writings. Embedded in the narratives of Black women's writings is a poetics of the natural world, a poetics that enables Black women's subjectivities to be reimagined.[1] Hurston, Walker, and Brand embrace the conflation "woman" and "nature" in their novels, but they depart from the reductive notion of woman as "mother nature" and instead present Black women's engagement and identification with the natural world as liberatory and as a means to transcend circumscribed notions of Black womanhood. I intentionally employ classic texts to advance a new intervention and position natural world writing as a part of Black women's theoretical savviness and creativity. By engaging Hurston's and Walker's canonical novels and Brand's more recent text, the uninvestigated presences of ecofeminist engagement with Black women's writings are illuminated and call attention to contemporary texts that bring that legacy forward. Walker's homage to Hurston is clear, and it is one she acknowledges.[2] Brand's novel implicitly engages Hurston and Walker and functions as an intertextual testament to the rich legacy of Black women's natural world writings, one that is both contemporary and diasporic. When juxtaposed, these novels demonstrate the possibilities for nuanced comparative analyses of Afro-diasporic women's writings and serve a reminder that comparisons can be made without eliding differences, comparisons that heed Carole Boyce-Davies and Molara Ogundipe-Leslie's call to learn to listen to the specificities of Black women's speech (7).

This chapter bridges the discourse on Black women writers' self-representation strategies and literary ecocriticism to illustrate how such writers as Hurston, Walker, and Brand articulate Black womanhood and sexuality through ecocentric language and natural world imagery. Like Spencer, they revision natural world imagery, and I argue that their use of natural imagery is powerful symbolism through which they map their own contours of a self-fashioned womanhood and implicitly invite other Black women to do the same. In doing so, they transcend oppressive, circumscribed notions of womanhood. And, here, I want to return to Carla L. Peterson's reminder that Black women's bodies are perpetually (mis)interpreted and are imbued with a historical legacy that renders them grotesque ("Foreword" x–xi). Thus, this self-representation is necessary.

While this chapter argues that Hurston, Walker, and Brand deploy their environmental consciousness to articulate Black womanhood, I do not intend to argue that they envision the same Black womanhood. Hurston, Walker, and Brand draw on nature as a metonym for what is beautiful, stable, and normative; however, they are not interested in reproducing and mobilizing the norm. The juxtaposition of an environmental conscious-ness and Black women's sexuality offers the possibility of reading Black women's sexuality in noncorporeal ways. This decorporealization of the Black female body and emphasis on the soul or the mind is a strategy of bodily representation that such writers as Frances E. W. Harper and Pau-line Hopkins turned to in the nineteenth century in an attempt to reclaim the always-exploited Black woman's body. As Deborah McDowell explains, "The nineteenth century was a watershed era for black women's recovery of their bodies from discourses that functioned historically to consign them to the realm of the 'serviceable corporeal'" ("Afterword" 299). This empha-sis on nonphysical attributes shifted focus away from Black women's bodies as repositories for sexual and racial violence and presented Black women as agents and complex human beings. Thus, Hurston, Walker, and Brand are summoning a long-standing tradition of Black women's rhetorical resis-tance by suggesting that Black women's subjectivities are not exclusively corporeal. In doing so, I suggest that using an ecoliterary lens facilitates the listening that Davies and Ogundipe-Leslie call for and enables readers to discuss the discursive strategies through which their characters create the contours of their own visions of womanhood. Exploring the connec-tions between the natural world symbolisms and Black womanhood allows readers to identify a common ground between Janie, Celie, and Elizete and examine the ways that, though in Florida, rural Georgia, and the Caribbean and Canada, respectively, they still "fight the same old men" and reimagine and redefine the contours of their womanhood by drawing on images of the natural world (Shange, *A Daughter's Geography* 21).

A central image that Walker, Hurston, and Brand share is that of trees, and in each of their novels, trees figure strongly in the development of their female protagonists.[3] Given this association with trauma, ecocriticism and ecopoetics may seem like unlikely pairings for Black women's writings. Critics Karla Armbruster and Kathleen R. Wallace caution against such a categorical dismissal, arguing that the complete negation of nonwhite, non-male-authored texts perpetuates myths of the natural world: "If ecocriti-cism limits itself to the study of one genre—the personal narrative of the Anglo-American [male] nature writing tradition—or to one physical land-scape—the ostensibly untrammeled American wilderness—it risks seriously misrepresenting the significance of multiple natural and built environments to writers with other ethnic, national, or racial affiliations" (7).

One of the most iconic uses of tree imagery is found in *Their Eyes Were Watching God,* when sixteen-year-old Janie Crawford experiences a transcendent sexual, spiritual awakening and consciousness-gaining moment under a pear tree. Literary critic Gurleen Grewal begins her analysis by pointing to this moment, underscoring its centrality not only within the novel itself but within the literary canon: "This remains one of the most captivating epiphanies in literature, sensuously describing the felt spirituality of the cosmos in a knowing that is intuitive and direct" (104). The image of the tree is a powerful symbol throughout the novel for Janie because her existential experience is also a deeply spiritual and sensual one in which she is awakened to the beauty of the natural world:

> She was stretched on her back beneath the pear tree soaking in the alto chant of the visiting bees, the gold of the sun and the panting breath of the sea breeze when the inaudible voice of it all came to her. She saw a dust-bearing bee sink into the sanctum of a bloom; the thousand sister-calyxes arch to meet the love embrace and the ecstatic shiver of the tree from root to tiniest branch creaming in ever blossom and frothing with delight. So this was a marriage! She had been summoned to behold a revelation. . . . Oh to be a pear tree—*any* tree in bloom! With kissing bees singing of the beginning of the world! (10, 11)

Prominent interpretations of Janie's pear tree point to the importance of this moment in Janie's life and the trajectory of the novel, but this is not the first time she invokes tree imagery. Equally important as a close reading of this moment, is asking *why* the pear tree and *what* it tells us about how Janie is theorizing and reimagining her gender and sexuality, and this interrogation of how an individual theorizes and articulates their relationship to the natural world is the analytical work ecopoetics seeks to perform. Just as Spencer's intertwined writing and gardening practices were acts of self-preservation and self-creation, Janie's identification with the pear tree is also an act of self-creation. What I am arguing here is that in creating the pear tree, Janie also creates herself. A Spencerian analysis enables us to see the artistry and theoretical underpinnings of Janie's self-creation.[4]

We see Janie's theorizing taking place in the second chapter of the novel, as she likens her life experiences to a tree: "Janie saw her life like a great tree in leaf with the things suffered, things enjoyed, things done and undone. Dawn and doom was in the branches" (8). Janie's identification with a tree takes place before she begins to explain to Pheoby why she has returned, noticeably without Tea Cake and visibly distressed. Pheoby invites her to share her story, and it is before she begins her storytelling that she makes this connection. This identification is significant because it illustrates that

Janie is making meaning of her life experiences. That the image she summons is a tree not only suggests that is she able to map the cartographies of her pain; it also reveals a sense of self-preservation and resilience because she summons an image that is aesthetically beautiful, rooted, and unfettered.

Janie's experience under the pear tree extends beyond a coming-of-age because she also develops a self-consciousness that awakens her both sexually and spiritually, and this awakening persists throughout her life. It is also important to remember that Janie is explaining to Pheoby why she has returned, so she is tasked with the challenge of where to begin her narrative. That she begins her story with this consciousness-gaining moment under a pear tree is a powerful declaration of her subjectivity, one that also enables Janie to articulate her sexuality on her own terms. Pheoby and the townspeople are curious about Tea Cake and want to hear the story of a romantic failure; however, Janie asserts her narrative agency and begins the story of rebirth, a moment in which she came into her own consciousness and her imagination. Similar to Shug Avery's locating God in the natural world, Janie is awakened to the divine both within nature and within herself. This acknowledgment of the divine within herself is a profound affirmation and meditation that guides the course of Janie's life, as she relentlessly protects her internal vision of divinity. This moment serves as significant reframing of her life, and she engages in a kind of corrective history by beginning with the pear tree. That Janie summons a tree image again—this time to begin a story—sends the message that her life cannot be reduced to isolated incidents. In other words, her narrative cannot be reduced to Tea Cake and narrow assumptions about her sexuality.

As Janie walks into town in overalls, the townspeople are curious as to why she has returned, but this curiosity immediately shifts to a policing of her sexuality with comments suggesting that Janie is carrying herself in a way that is neither age-appropriate nor respectable. While her sexuality is being policed, she is also being sexualized, and one of the townspeople remarks: "What she doin coming back here in dem overhalls? Cant she find no dress to put on? . . . What dat ole forty year old 'oman doin' wid her hair swingin' down her back lak some young gal?" (2). In this moment, Janie's body is on display and becomes the object of a violent, sexual gaze, with men "saving with the mind what they lost with the eye" (2). Her experience can be likened to Saartjie Baartman's, as her body becomes a site of desire, grotesquerie, and jealousy. When juxtaposed with the townspeople policing and projecting Janie's sexuality, her deployment of a tree to describe her life becomes an act through which engages in "unmirroring" and represents her body and sexuality in accordance with her internal vision (Hobson 89). Here, I draw on Janell Hobson's use of "unmirroring," which she describes as the process through which Black women struggle for subjectivity and "constantly grate against the distorted images of the dominant culture" (89). However, Janie's use of this tree is not to suggest that she is attempting to mobilize her body and her sexuality as what is normal. Instead, Janie's turning to a tree to define herself symbolizes her right to name her sexuality as she chooses. Janie's tree is just that: *it is her tree*. And this tree is "half her world," to borrow a Spencerian idiom. The collective gaze upon Janie's body suggests that she is both deviant and "unnatural"; however, by aligning herself with this tree imagery that she conjures, Janie performs a radical act of self-care and simultaneously clings to her self-fashioned womanhood and rejects conventional definitions of what is normative. Her use of the tree also evokes the decorporealizing strategies that Black female authors have used in their effort to reclaim Black women's sexualities. Thus, part of what Janie is doing with the tree is suggesting that there is more to her than just her physical attributes, and her sexuality is not exclusively tied to her physical body.

Gurleen Grewal argues that the tree symbol for Janie also has existential value for her and functions as "a vision of Life that becomes a blueprint for the soul's quest" (104). Thus, in the ethereal, consciousness-gaining moment, Janie is both affirmed, as she sees herself reflected in the tree, and she is given the language with which to articulate her "inner vision" (103). This inner vision is what guides Janie throughout the novel, and she is propelled by an unrelenting desire to protect and achieve this vision. We see this protection and self-preservation articulated when Nanny informs Janie that she will be marrying Logan Killicks: "The vision of Logan Killicks was desecrating the pear tree, but Janie didn't know how to tell Nanny that. She merely hunched over and pouted at the floor" (13). Janie is coerced into this marriage and must acquiesce, but her acknowledgment that Logan Killicks "desecrates" the pear tree is her recognizing that he is not compatible with her vision of herself. The tree enables Janie to visualize a Black womanhood beyond the bounds of Nanny's and Eatonville's prescriptive mores; it offers her the opportunity to free herself. By clinging to an image of a tree, Janie symbolically clings to her own notions of womanhood.

Images of the natural world follow her throughout her marriage to Killicks and into second marriage to Joe "Jody" Starks. She compares her marriage to Killicks to a stump in the woods and her sex life with Jody to "no longer a daisy-field" (20, 67). These images of the natural world serve as an internal compass for her, and though she is not able to re-create the moment under the pear tree with these men, the language she inherits from that moment instills in her the knowledge of what a healthy relationship for her should be: "Janie's perception of the cosmic tree of beauty offers an epistemology and blueprint for all relationships" (Grewal 104). It is her clinging to this vision that ultimately leads her to Tea Cake, the man who "could be a bee to a blossom—a pear tree blossom in the spring," and for the first time in her life she is able to experience being a tree (101). As Scott Hicks explains, Janie not only re-creates this feeling again, but also her union with Tea Cake enables her to *become* a tree: "In the end, Janie becomes the tree she loves, as her marriage to Vergible 'Tea Cake' Woods names her Janie Woods. . . . 'Hurston merges the two, making Janie a human/tree hybrid'" (Hicks 119). Tea Cake indeed equips Janie with the practical skill of learning to shoot, which enables her to save her own life by killing him. However, by helping her to become the tree she has always desired, Tea Cake enables her to embody the poetics of her tree and teaches Janie "the maiden language all over" (109). Thus, the legacy of their relationship is not just that Janie experiences love and sexual pleasure for the first time. Rather, it is that with Tea Cake she is able to symbolically embody the tree she desires, and she is able to learn the language and the poetics with which to articulate her Black womanhood.

It is this language that enables her to share her story with Pheoby, and what we see in Janie through the telling of her story is that she does not say what she could have said rather succinctly. The opportunity to tell her story—the story of her Black womanhood—in her own words is freeing, and it is Pheoby who helps her: "Pheoby's hungry listening helped Janie to tell her story" (10). Pheoby's patient ear models the kind of listening Carole Boyce-Davies and Molara Ogundipe-Leslie advocate for Black women, so Janie's liberation is illustrative of the kind of liberation Black women can experience when granted the opportunity to be heard: "How do black women get heard? By assertively and bold-facedly transgressing the imposed boundaries; by being insistent, supportive; by speaking constantly directly or indirectly, though in multiple forms but always demanding hearing; by challenging the pretended disabilities of hearing; by constantly creating" (9). Ultimately Janie's story is about a woman's liberation through storytelling. Janie's ability, as a Black woman, to name her life *and* her body as spaces deserving of sexual and existential pleasure and making this her quest is a crucial intervention, as Black women's bodies historically have been sites of sexual violence. That Janie's liberation comes through storytelling underscores that her pear tree gives her the poetics with which to articulate her womanhood and tell this story because she frames her narrative around the image of the tree, and the purpose of her quest is to find a way to live and embody the poetics of the tree. By preserving and protecting this image of the tree, Janie preserves and protects herself.

Janie's representation is also important because not only is she a Black woman asserting herself as a sexual subject, but also she is a *childless* woman asserting herself as such. A peculiar aspect of the novel is that she has been married three times, does not bear any children, and nobody discusses this in the novel. This would have been quite unconventional in the 1930s milieu in which Hurston was writing, but Janie represents a womanhood in which women's sexuality is separate from women's procreation. That Janie's childlessness is not mentioned (even by the jealous townspeople in their criticism and surveillance) can be interpreted as a commentary against conflating motherhood and womanhood and as an important departure from colonial narratives that associated Black women's bodies with obligatory biological and economic forms of reproductive labor. We can also interpret Janie's childlessness as an act of self-care through which she intentionally prioritizes her sexual subjectivity over the confines of domesticity and motherhood. Janie *does* give birth and create; she creates herself. The aperture that is formed in Janie's particular articulation of sexual subjectivity and journey of self-creation is one that also expands the definition of womanhood, wresting it away from biological notions of motherhood.

Janie's clinging to the image of the tree reminds us, as Katherine McKittrick argues, "how bodily geography can be" (46). By creating a definition of womanhood that stems from a tree, Janie is able to expand her geographical options and escape the "territorializing" that is imposed on Black women's bodies. McKittrick explains: "Once the racial-sexual body is territorialized, it is marked as decipherable and knowable—as subordinate, inhumane, rape-able, deviant, procreative, placeless" (45). By using the poetics of the natural world to articulate her womanhood, Janie is able to resist this territorializing of her body and find refuge in an image of a pear tree that allows her to imagine a womanhood without boundaries. Though Janie experiences the consciousness-waking moment under a pear tree at her grandmother's home, she does not want to be *that* pear tree; she simply wants to be a tree—*any tree* (10; emphasis added). That the tree she desires is metaphorical and not literal is also illustrative of the way Janie is able to imagine herself beyond the bounds of prescriptive womanhood. This metaphorical tree illustrates that she understands that her womanhood and sexuality can be of her own fashioning and that this self-fashioning is limitless. By being *her* tree, Janie also creates a blank canvas for herself because, though she conjures an image from the natural world, it exists in her imagination and is free from aforementioned colonial legacies. Thus, by summoning an image of a tree, what Janie is doing is both embarking on a project of self-liberation and theorizing the possibilities of a womanhood predicated on the poetics of the natural world and negotiating a space to exist.

Looking at her vagina for the first time, Celie describes her vagina as a rose: "Then my pussy lips be black. Then inside look like a wet rose" (78). Critics have frequently read Celie's sexuality through the lens of lesbianism and Walker's conception of womanism, readings that are valid but only provide partial insight into how Celie theorizes her womanhood. Ecopoetics provides a nuanced critical departure from traditional readings, and just as with Janie's pear tree, it facilitates a reading that analyzes not just *what* the wet rose means but *why* specifically the wet rose is used as a figuration for a Black woman's vagina. The image of a wet rose symbolizes Celie's sexually aroused vagina and newfound sexual pleasure upon discovering her clitoris. In likening Celie's vagina to a wet rose, Walker arguably signals the color purple itself, which could signify the woman(ist)-centered nature of the novel and Celie's sexuality. Linda Abbandonato explains: "But most daringly significant is the use of the color purple to encode the specifically feminine *jouissance* experienced by Celie. Associated with Easter and resurrection, and thus with spiritual regeneration, purple may also evoke the female genitalia; indeed, Walker makes the color connection explicit in 'One Child of One's Own' by provocatively describing a black woman's vagina as 'the color of raspberries and blackberries—or scuppernongs and muscadines'" (1113). That Walker likens Celie's vagina to a wet rose is a profound reclamation of not only Celie's body but also Black women's bodies. As a victim of repeated acts of sexual and physical assault, Celie's body is a site of both historical and present trauma. Walker's associating Black women's genitalia with the regal color of resurrection and the uncorrupted beauty of the natural world allows Black women's bodies to be reimagined beyond narratives of trauma. Celie's locating of her "button" is arguably the first of many steps she will take toward asserting herself as sexual subject, and Shug's guidance symbolically illustrates that a new narrative about women's bodies has been created. That Shug, as a sexually liberated Black woman, is supporting Celie's expression of sexuality is a critical moment of Black female community building both within the text and within the tradition of Black female literature, one that Christopher S. Lewis argues serves as a "model of sexual vulnerability and mutual dependence that has them working together consensually toward self-love rather than relating hierarchically—an interaction different from Albert's masculinist relationship with Celie" (163).

The Color Purple is a kind of culmination of the apertures created when Black women's ecological materialities are considered. In the same way that the novel concludes with a utopic reunion, its rich tapestry of Black female characters represents a kind of utopic reunion in and of itself because a new, liberated Black community is present at the end of the novel, one that celebrates a freedom of thought and sexuality and a decentering of heteronormative behavior and hegemonic patriarchy. The self-fashioned individuality represented in such characters as Celie, Nettie, Sofia, and Shug Avery is apparent and is illustrative of the range and complexity Hurston called for in her critical essay "What White Publishers Won't Print."[5] The relationship between Celie and Shug Avery is a particularly significant one because it is through Shug Avery's nurturing that Celie discovers her sexuality and asserts her sexual subjectivity. The queerness of their relationship creates a space for the expression of nonheteronormative sexualities and allows for heteronormativity to be decentered both within Celie's life and the novel.

It is through the language of the natural world that this queerness is articulated, and we see this when Celie first sets eyes on Shug: "She look so stylish it like the trees all round the house draw themself up tall for a better look" (45). That Celie claims Shug's attractiveness is so striking that trees move in obeisance is both a powerful affirmation of Black female beauty and a bold declaration of her own sexual desire. This moment is one of the first times in the novel where Celie articulates and experiences sexual desire. By likening Shug's appeal to trees, what Celie does in this moment is align her erotic desire and Shug's beauty with the natural world. Celie is careful to note that the trees shifted in response to Shug's presence, and this shifting is symbolic of the decentering of hegemonic masculinity and heterosexuality that takes place throughout the novel. Through this analogy of shifting trees, Celie simultaneously critiques what is traditionally viewed as natural and positions both her queerness and Shug's allure as harmonious and compatible with nature.

Walker invokes *Their Eyes Were Watching God* throughout the novel, and one of the most poignant homages to Hurston is her symbolic use of tree imagery. Similar to Janie, Celie possesses an affinity for and identification with trees, and we learn early on in the novel that she summoned tree imagery to cope with the trauma of the physical, sexual, and psychological abuse Mr.—inflicts upon her: "I make myself wood. I say to myself, Celie, you a tree. That's how come I know trees fear man" (22). The reader is not aware of Celie's queerness at this point; however, we must remember Celie is, yet she lacks the language to name her desire. Thus, we may also read this disassociation strategy and making herself wood as a Celie's attempt to save her sexuality for the partner she desires. What is crucial to note about making herself wood is that she is transforming herself into a hard, impenetrable object. This strategy symbolically shields Celie from the unwanted sexual intercourse, both past and present, thus enabling her to reimagine and reclaim her body as a virginal space.

By asserting that she is a tree, Celie, like Janie, is protecting her internal vision of herself and engaging in a radical act of self-care and self-preservation. She is embarking on a path of self-creation. The image of a tree gives Celie a sense of rootedness and grounding, which she profoundly lacks in her life. In this way, Celie's conjuring of this tree image can be read as her attempt to make meaning of her life and rewrite her narrative. It is this grounding that enables Celie to transcend both the immediate moment of unwanted sex and the past traumas and narratives thrust upon her body; she grounds herself in order to transcend. When juxtaposed, the aforementioned scenes function as a confirmation of Celie's internal vision and sense of self. Celie becomes a tree to protect herself from sexual abuse and to preserve her sexuality, and it is crucial to remember that it is the image of trees shifting that she invokes to describe Shug's stylishness and desirability. Thus, we can read the symbolism of the trees bending forward to gaze at Shug as a metaphor for Celie's latent sexual desire. In other words, it is Shug who awakens Celie's desire and draws it out of secrecy; Shug is the catalyst for the shift. The rigid, impervious wood-tree imagery she once summoned to envision herself is now freely yielding to Shug, and we can read this moment as a foreshadowing of the trajectory of their relationship.

It is this new narrative and the symbolic resurrection that takes place that allow both Shug and Celie to reimagine and redefine virginity in such a way that Celie can be considered a virgin:

Yall make love any better? she ast.
    Us try, I say. He try to play with the button but feel like his fingers dry. Us don't git nowhere much.
    You still a virgin? she ast.
    I reckon. I say. (110)

Celie and Shug are not just redefining virginity; they are also critiquing and questioning the inherent value of virginity. This critique is particularly important, considering the renderings of Black women's bodies as fixed, exploitable natural resources. This rendering is what Janie's grandmother is alluding to when she says, "De nigger woman is de mule uh de world so fur as Ah can see" (14). Celie and Shug's critique of virginity functions as a rebuttal to Nanny's pessimistic appraisal, and they symbolically reject this designation. The aforementioned invoking of the resurrection is emblematic of what the discovery of her clitoris represents for Celie. Shug's encouraging Celie to look at her vagina in the mirror and helping her find her "button" is far more significant than a mere anatomical lesson, and it can be likened to Pheoby's "hungry listening" that helps Janie heal. Shug helps Celie look at her own body through her own eyes and reminds her that her body is *hers,* she may use it how she pleases, and she is entitled to sexual pleasure. Thus, what Shug helps Celie do is inscribe meaning into her own body, and this enables her to resist the insidious shaming that women must endure. As Melissa Harris-Perry explains: "Shame works through real or anticipated social sanctions that punish violations of group rules and thus helps us stay within the lines of acceptable behavior and thought. . . . Shaming is a problem of consistent and intentional misrecognition" (107, 122). This rejection of shame is what enables Celie to reimagine "the four categories in which Albert places her when she responds to his insults with a final declaration: 'I'm pore, I'm black, I may be ugly and can't cook, a voice say to everything listening. But I'm here.' . . . She shamelessly embraces the terms Albert intended as insults [and] . . . finds a means of articulating her experiences in the face of extreme degradation" (Lewis 164). We may read this profound reimagining as further confirmation of Celie's groundedness, and it is indicative of her relationship with the land. This declaration reifies her protective mantra, "Celie, you a tree," because she embodies the rootedness of a tree as she articulates her hereness, a hereness that is simultaneously rooted and unfettered. In this scene, she is articulating her humanity and her understanding of her positionality, and she is doing it such a way that transcends and reimagines the misnaming and unmirroring Albert enacts. Rooted in the vision of her tree-self, Celie is able to transcend the shaming and false narratives imposed upon her.

Katherine McKittrick is acutely aware of the ecopoetics in Dionne Brand's work, and she makes this clear in the opening line of her book *Demonic Grounds:* "When Dionne Brand writes, she writes the land" (ix). In *In Another Place, Not Here,* Dionne Brand's protagonist, Elizete, "writes the land" as she draws upon natural world symbols to articulate her womanhood, and similar to Janie, she utilizes the poetics of the natural world to express her desires. Brand's novel opens with Elizete working in a sugarcane field and experiencing a love-at-first-sight moment when she sees her soon-to-be lover, Verlia, a woman she likens to "a drink of cool water" (3). Musing about her lover, Elizete creates a description saturated with natural world imagery: "I abandon everything for Verlia. I sink in Verlia and let she flesh swallow me up. I devour she. She open me up like any morning. Limp, limp and rain light, soft to the marrow. She make me wet. She tongue scorching like the hot sun. I love that shudder between her legs, love the plain wash and see of her, the swell and bloom of her softness. And is all. And if is all I could do on the earth, is all" (5). Elizete's assertion that Verlia opened her up like the morning suggests that Verlia brings her into sensory-filled consciousness and reveals a part of herself that she did not know existed. Elizete explains her leaving Isaiah as the moment she "turn woman," and this evokes both a sexual awakening and a coming into self-consciousness, a rebirth of sorts (4). However, what Elizete experiences is more intimate; she experiences sexual desire for the first time and is able to assert herself as a sexual subject: "Everything make sense from then the way flesh make sense settling into blood. I think to myself how I must be sleeping all this time. I must be was in a trance because it was as if Verl wake me up to say, 'Girl put on your clothes. Let we go now'" (6). Thus, through her relationship with Verlia, Elizete is able to unleash the power of her erotic. That everything makes sense to Elizete and she is able to name previously unspeakable feelings captures Audre Lorde's notion of the erotic as the "power of our unexpressed or unrecognizable feeling . . . [and] measure between the beginnings of our sense of self and the chaos of our strongest feelings" (53, 54).

Notice that Elizete already possessed this language of the natural world. The novel follows a nonchronological pattern, Kristina Quynn argues, that is both "woman oriented and queer" and "coordinates [with] Elizete's changing sense of self" (127). Because of this nonlinear pattern, we learn after Elizete meets Verlia that Elizete's drawing upon the natural world is something she has done since she was a child, and she closely identifies with nature, especially samaan trees: "Under the samaan tree is where I grow up. It was wide and high and the light between what it leave of the sky was soft and it look like a woman with hands in the air. A samaan is a tree with majesty and I think of this samaan as my mother. She wave from far and the sun pass through she, and she was my keeper. Until the woman I was given to come home from the field the samaan was my mother" (17). Before we consider the significance of Elizete's naming the samaan tree as her mother, it is important to analyze this passage alongside her description of Verlia. This passage confirms that Elizete indeed had the language of the natural world available to her, but it was not until she met Verlia that she was able to mobilize this speech and use it to describe her own desires. This speech remained dormant and sequestered. This section of the novel is entitled "Elizete, beckoned," so this elicits the question of what or whom might be beckoning her. While we may draw a connection to Verlia's beauty and the impending relationship that beckons her, we can also think about the poetics of the natural world beckoning her into speech. This poetics not only gives Elizete the ability to articulate Verlia's beauty, but also it gives her the ability to name her desires. She is able to ascribe speech to her erotics.

That Elizete names a samaan tree as her mother is a significant project of self-definition. Though she is an orphan, she disregards this category and chooses to rewrite her narrative, and she begins by constructing a new genealogy for herself. This new genealogy endows her with a sense of identity, one that gives her a sense of rootedness. As Paul Huebener and Dionne Brand explain, this grounding is something that sets her apart from her enslaved great-great-great-grandmother, Adela, who resisted any identification with her new Caribbean island home: "That her relationship with the samaan is nurturing enough for her to think of it as a mother-daughter relationship allows Elizete to overcome the inability that afflicts Adela—caul drawn over her eyes—to be fully born into this place. A familial relation with her surroundings turns Elizete into what Adela was not: a named, seeing, feeling person with a sense of relatedness and belonging" (619). What enables Elizete to experience this relatedness and belonging is her connection to the natural world, and she establishes this connection by naming. Though Elizete claims that she names for Adela's sake and as an act of obeisance, what she is also doing is negotiating space for herself to exist. She is theorizing the geographical possibilities of her existence, and through naming she simultaneously creates and defines new spaces. Thus, Elizete's naming this tree as her mother is a powerful statement through which she is not only articulating a desire for such freedom but also claiming it as her birthright. Naming the samaan tree as her mother also reflects a desire for sexual freedom. Elizete describes the samaan tree as a woman whose hands are extended (17). The image of a woman whose hands are unfettered and outstretched is a symbol of freedom, determination, and possibility. Like

Janie's and Celie's trees, Elizete's tree also represents a project of erotic self-fashioning and self-creation. That Elizete genders her tree and names it as woman signals that love for women is essential in her life because this image not only represents a desired matrilineal heritage; it also reveals how central a woman's love is within her life.

Just as Janie utilizes the vision of her pear tree as means of self-preservation during her abusive marriages, Elizete turns to the natural world as a form of escape during her compulsory relationship with Isaiah; however, it is not an image of her samaan tree–mother that comes into her mind. Recalling their sexual intercourse, Elizete reveals that she fixates on thoughts of wood lice to escape the trauma of sex with Isaiah:

> These times I wander, I turn my head to the wall and travel in the dust tunnels of wood lice. I cover my self in their fine, fine sand, I slide through the tunnel and I see all where I have to go, and I try to reach where they live and I try to be like them because try as I did when I was little I never see one of them yet only the rifts on the walls. Is so they work in secret and in their own company. Is so I travel the walls of this room catching hell and Isaiah' advantage till morning. (10–11)

That Elizete fantasizes about being a wood louse reveals a latent desire for autonomy. Earlier in the novel she reveals just how little geographic freedom she has while working for Isaiah: "I born to clean Isaiah' house and work can since I was a child and say what you want Isaiah feed me and all I have to do is lay down under him at night and work the cane in the day" (4). In addition to revealing the cartographies of her struggle, Elizete is also sharing what Katherine McKittrick calls a "shape of mystery" (39). McKittrick uses this terminology to refer to the "mapping of the terror and transparency of slave spaces," and though she is specifically referring to conditions under slavery, what Elizete experiences while working for Isaiah is a form of bondage (39). Like the wood lice, Elizete is confined to a small space while she is bound to Isaiah. However, her fixation and desire to be like the wood lice stems from their having a geographic freedom that she envies; though they inhabit small spaces, their mobility is unrestricted and they can avoid detection.

Elizete is having these fantasies while engaging in heterosexual intercourse with Isaiah because this is not the type of relationship she desires. The images of wood lice are a survival strategy, one that enables her to disassociate from and reject her obligatory heterosexual relationship and preserve her queerness. Like Celie's tree, Elizete's wood lice image becomes her protective mantra. The same imagery that enables her to preserve her queerness also enables her to articulate her sexual desire freely. As she describes the moment Isaiah catches her making love to Verlia, she invokes the natural world, and it is this imagery that allows her to articulate sexual pleasure: "I didn't even raise my head. I finished loving Verlia taking she face and she skin black as water in my hand so I was to remember what I lose something for" (5). Again, she likens Verlia to water, underscoring that not only is Verlia essential to her but also that Verlia is able to satiate her in a way that Isaiah simply cannot. By likening Verlia to water, Brand is able to question and destabilize what is traditionally deemed natural. That Elizete's queerness is exclusively expressed through natural world imagery enables Brand to decenter heterosexuality and undermine traditional literary eco-critical readings that view the environment through a heteronormative lens. Elizete and Verlia's relationship posits the natural world as a vehicle through which queer love and queerness can be imagined and expressed. Their queer love also engages the idea of communal, expansive mothering, and suggests that the things that come from Black women's bodies are not just commodities. Verlia's ability to nurture Elizete into a sexual subject and elicit sexual pleasure from Elizete's body engages this idea of communal mothering because she is able to help Elizete tap into the power of her erotic and redefine her body as a site of sexual pleasure.

Working with Spencer's poetry and experiencing her archive has taught me to listen to Black women's poetics on their terms. When we examine the ecopoetics in Black women's writings, it becomes possible to read Janie's, Celie's, and Elizete's trees as powerful symbols of self-fashioned woman-hood and budding self-consciousness through which they are defining their sexuality and womanhood on their own terms. These images are radical acts of self-care through which Janie, Celie, Elizete can fashion and preserve notions of Black womanhood that align with their internal visions. Thus, it becomes possible to read Janie's quest to re-create the moment under the pear tree, Celie's wet rose, and Elizete's claiming a samaan tree as her mother as symbols through which they may assert their erotic self-fashioning and self-creation. The trees symbolize that these women are both grounded in their *hereness*—their individual Black womanhood, their sexuality, their humanity—and able to transcend. Since what is natural is traditionally utilized to mobilize normativities, what emerges from Hurston's, Walker's, and Brand's novels is a poetics of the natural world through which the authors can also question what is natural. In doing so, heteronormativity is decentered, so childlessness and queerness are not deemed deviant; instead, they signal the endless possibilities and ways of being for Black womanhood.

Hurston, Walker, and Brand not only articulate their own environmental appreciation, but also they establish themselves as "ecovisionary artists" and map the experiences of Black womanhood onto the natural world.[6] By envisioning female characters whose womanhood is expressed through the natural world, Hurston, Walker, and Brand position both themselves and their Black female characters as "agents whose imaginations are not limited by the stimuli of oppression but whose intellectual vibrancy is capable of negotiating domination and imaginative work outside of oppression's bounds" (Ruffin 16). The significant theorizing that is taking place in these novels is the theorizing of Black women's gender and sexuality, and Hurston, Walker, and Brand invite readers to explore the place of the natural world in Black women's writings and analyze Black women's ecological materialities. Revisiting the Spencerian question posed at the beginning of this chapter, what happens when we do not separate Black women from their gardens is that we are able to bear witness to how they self-create and theorize. Black women's literature may be "the last place thought of" as a site for ecocritical analysis, but Hurston's, Walker's, and Brand's works invite further inquiry into how Black women writers use natural world imagery to articulate their characters' shapes of mystery through ecopoetics.

Coda

"If People Were Like Flowers"

In one of her many notebooks, Anne Spencer wrote the following words: "If people were like flowers, an hour is all I'd ask of them—and you—if people were like flowers [?]"[1] Like much of her ephemeral writing, this quote is undated, and the manuscript is seemingly "incomplete." However, this quote beautifully encapsulates the sense of being Anne Spencer constructs through the natural world and is a testament to the fact that the natural world was the prism through which she viewed the world. In the middle of the quote, Spencer breaks and poses a question, one that invites us to participate in this kind of thinking. Spencer's work is both a gift and a daring theoretical intervention. She provides readers with the gift of her poetry and prose infused with natural world imagery and invites us to consider the natural world as a legitimate, yet unexplored, site of Black feminist epistemology, literary criticism, and ecocriticism. When Spencer's rhetorical contributions are unearthed, what emerges is a rhetoric of Black womanhood predicated on individuality, self-care, and happiness, a rhetoric that shaped her world.

Because single-author studies are now often discouraged in academia, it is imperative for me to talk about how my study of Anne Spencer has enriched my analysis of Black women's literary studies more generally. This work's contributions lie in its introduction of new archives for Black women's literary studies. First and foremost, it pushes against the negation of Black women's unconventional archives. The published, anthologized form of Spencer's work is a very stilted version, one that is both acutely aware of and anxious about the public gaze and consists of approximately thirty poems. Because of the unconventionality of her archive and her reluctance to publish, Spencer's writing falls prey to being overlooked. Showcasing her unknown works has enabled me to highlight the aspects of Spencer—"the creative spark[s]" (Walker, *Mothers' Gardens* 240)—that resist containment and push against the negation of Black women's unconventional archives. Spencer's unorthodox archive of unpublished, undated poems and prose written on ephemera and other materials is a rich text and space-making act in itself, one that beautifully illustrates the audacious eccentricity she embodied in her daily life. What I have suggested here is that it is not writing alone that sustained Spencer but also the process of how she wrote. Her archive exists because she carefully preserved the "'leventy-leven bits" of paper stuck in so many different places until her death in 1975, and her garden at 1313 Pierce Street in Lynchburg, Virginia, is also an archive and is a testament to the significance of the natural world in her life.

My study of Anne Spencer also introduces Black women's natural world writings as an unexplored archive for Black feminist thought. This perspective invites alternative readings of such periods and movements as the New Negro Renaissance and modernism that are framed around the Great Migration to the urban North and demonstrates that rural spaces were key sites of Black artistic expression and Black identity. And, here, I am explicitly engaging Stefanie K. Dunning's critique of romanticizing the urban, city-filled North as a racism-free "safe haven" responsible for birthing a modern, cosmopolitan Black individual (21–22). We do not usually think about Blackness and Black femaleness rendered through the natural world. Spencer was so deeply invested in thinking about being and humanity, and central to that thinking was the natural world, so her work is an invitation, an imperative to think about the place of the natural world in Black women's writings. This archive for Black feminist engagement offers another lens through which to understand how Black women theorize and articulate themselves, and Anne Spencer shows us that natural world writing is a part of Black women's theoretical savviness and creativity. By connecting the discourse of Black women's writing and literary ecocriticism, it is also possible to bear witness to the Black environmental imagination, an imagination whose existence has been negated, denied, and silenced throughout history. Furthermore, since what is natural is traditionally utilized to mobilize normativities, we can bear witness to the ways in which Black women writers destabilize what is considered "natural." This lens situates ecocritical readings as a new site of analysis for Black women's writings and queer studies.

I want to return to the myth of Black environmental apathy and the natural word as a white space because this project also refutes these pervasive narratives. These myths persist because dominant narratives about nature consider only a white perspective. Black writers like Spencer were quite forward-thinking and were "green" before it was fashionable. They were critical of industrialization and advocated an antidominion relationship with the natural world that positioned human beings as stewards, not owners, of the earth. They were far from apathetic; rather, they viewed environmentalism as an urgent moral imperative, one that was inextricably linked to racial equality. Their meditations serve as evidence that a Black environmental imagination exists and invite further study into how Black writers theorize the natural world. Their work shows that Black environmental thought exists—and that it matters.

In our contemporary moment, the myth of Black environmental apathy is especially dangerous because to claim that Black people are antienvironmental or antinature is tantamount to saying that Black people do not have the right to be outdoors. Such a statement justifies the hyperpolicing and surveillance of Black individuals, and we have countless examples, from Christian Cooper to Ahmaud Arbery, who were simply bird-watching and jogging, respectively, to illustrate how being Black and outdoors is life-threatening. This myth is also harmful because it negates the work of Black environmental activists and obscures our ability to identify environmental justice issues as racial equality issues. Black writers were able to name environmental concerns as racial ones, so this unexplored archive of thought is also an opportunity—and an invitation—to learn about the intersectional relationship between environmental and racial justice concerns.

It is clear that the natural world was central to Anne Spencer's thinking and her being; it was life-affirming and life-giving. Perhaps this is what her friends and colleagues admired so much and why they frequented her home-garden literary salon; they accepted her invitation to imagine, and they saw her garden as an archive of imagination. I read her garden as a kind of concrete poetry—a quilt of sorts—but it is also a supplemental archive to the institutional one that exists at the University of Virginia. Her garden as an alternative archive reveals the centrality of the natural world to her being, her writing, and her conception of the natural world is beyond narratives of dominion and trauma. This turn away from trauma is what I think is revolutionary about her garden. She redefined what the natural world could be for Black people. She was able to imagine a "Black woman's world," so to speak, through nature, one that offered an alternative future disentangled from trauma. And her connectedness to the natural world also enabled her to imagine a Black woman's God.

The title of this book is pulled from a letter from a 1951 letter from Georgia Douglas Johnson in which she writes, "I do not separate you from your garden, your elegant verse and your sure philosophy," and my research unearths the nuances of Spencer's writing and ideas when her garden, verse, and philosophy are juxtaposed.[2] When Johnson says she does not separate Spencer from her garden, this statement, in addition to functioning as a poignant imperative, is an affirmation of Spencer's womanhood. Thus, Johnson's statement can be restated as, *I do not separate you from yourself.*

There is truly no way to fully capture Anne Spencer's audacity, eccentricity, imagination, brilliance, and creativity on the page. Though the materials from her archive pulse throughout this writer and the pages of this text, the materiality of her archive and her home and garden should be experienced in person, so please visit the Anne Spencer House and Garden Museum in Lynchburg, Virginia, and the Papers of Anne Spencer and the Spencer Family at the University of Virginia. My hope is that this project has served as invitation for further inquiry into her work and Black women's natural world writings. And if this book has been anything, it has been my love letter to Anne Spencer.

So, I will end here, not with a conclusion but, instead, with an invitation from Spencer to imagine: "If people were like flowers, an hour is all I'd ask of them—and you—if people were like flowers [?]"[3] Amen.

Afterword

Lessons from Anne Spencer

Some people have been thriving while in quarantine. Baking bread. Gardening. Journaling. Enjoying cocktails and coffee dates over Zoom. I'm not one of those people, and I haven't been doing any of those things.

I'll be honest: I feel completely undone. I vacillate between moments of crippling panic and anxiety and just regular panic and anxiety. And fear. Lots of fear.

I've been struggling to remain focused, productive, and remember who I was—and the range of emotions I used to feel—before the pandemic. I have been turning to a particular poet, Anne Spencer (1882–1975), for guidance on how to navigate this moment. Her oeuvre is stunning and merits far more than the scant attention it has received, but I'm moved by the artistry that was her life.

Anne Spencer was a Black woman-writer-mother-wife-civil-rights-and-community activist-intellectual-librarian-environmentalist whose poetry is primarily associated with the New Negro Renaissance, but her writing career spanned more than seventy years and primarily contained undated, unpublished prose written on ephemera. Her Lynchburg, Virginia, home that she shared with her husband, Edward, served as one of the three major literary salons during the New Negro Renaissance where she hosted the likes of W. E. B. Du Bois and James Weldon Johnson. Her home and garden still stand today and are recognized as a historical museum.

Indeed, Anne Spencer, the unsung New Negro Renaissance poet-activist, was a remarkable woman. But, for me, it is her self-care practice that I find most compelling.

Her daily routine consisted of rising at eleven in the morning, bathing for one hour, followed by brushing her hair for two hours, and spending the afternoon and evening gardening and writing until the wee hours of the morning.

It's easy to dismiss this as an "undisciplined" schedule and assume that Anne Spencer lived a privileged life. However, we must remember that she was a Black woman living in the South under the watchful eye of Jim Crow only one generation removed from slavery. What appears on the surface to be a leisurely schedule is a Black woman carefully and meticulously ordering her day in the way she sees fit.

During a time in which Black people were policed, surveilled, and told which spaces to occupy, here is a woman whose ethos was predicated on caring for herself and cultivating pleasure. Spencer was being how she wanted to be.

I marvel at her glorious audacity.

Spencer, of course, was also a writer. Though she's credited as a poet, much of her writing is prose. And she wrote on everything and about everything. She was always writing. When I visited her papers at the University of Virginia, I was struck by the myriad objects she transformed into canvases for writings: a packet of seeds, the top of a shoebox, Edward's accounting ledgers.

Yet, she wasn't concerned with publishing. Some of her writings are what I like to call "legibly illegible" because it's unlikely that anyone other than Spencer could read them. They are fragmentary in nature, and in many cases, her handwriting deviates from traditional prose logic and assumes a graphic quality with words cascading from various angles. Perhaps this illegibility was intentional. Perhaps it was the result of aging or arthritis in her hands.

Though she was constantly writing, she loathed publication. The published poems that we do have mostly came at the solicitations of friends. Her writing was autonomously hers and didn't exist for others' consumption.

This is a woman for whom writing was as essential as air, and I firmly believe that Spencer wrote not only to save her own life but also to create it.

I first encountered Anne Spencer's work as a graduate student, and she soon became the focus of my scholarly endeavors and personal admiration. I was writing about a woman who radically took care of herself and cultivated pleasure while I was barely sleeping and miserable. The irony. And perhaps that is why I was—and still am—drawn to her, especially now. In her ninety-three years, she lived through the major wars of the twentieth century with her son, Chauncey Spencer, serving in—and integrating—the U.S. Air Force during World War II. She, too, intimately experienced the pandemic that is structural racism.

Like Spencer, I am a Black woman living in a time when my very existence is considered a threat punishable by death. And simply stating that my life matters incites rage.

I read Spencer's daily routine as a bold declaration that her Black life mattered to her, and it was a beautiful affront to the Jim Crow system that attempted to rob African Americans of their personhood and dignity. To insist on the value of one's life and declare that one has the right to live freely is a radical act, and Spencer did just that.

As an artist, Spencer was not productive in the conventional sense; she never published a volume of poetry or prose. (Like many other female New Negro Renaissance writers, Spencer faced criticism that her poetry lacked a strong racial orientation and was too "feminine.") However, this was not due to a lack of talent or discipline. Her archive easily contains thousands of poems. She simply did not want to.

I admire Anne Spencer because she was brave enough to be the kind of Black woman she wanted—no, needed—to be. She kept "business hours" that worked for her. The metrics of publication did not work for her, so she crafted her own metrics and allowed herself to write to and for herself.

She set the terms through which she wanted to be legible. She allowed herself to be and fashioned a world in which she was valued.

Spencer dared to imagine and create a Black woman's world, and I honor her by trying to do the same.

Like her, I want to live life on my own terms and care for and about myself daily. I need to, especially now.

I aspire to marvel at my own glorious audacity.

I won't be baking bread during this pandemic or waking up at 6:00 a.m. to write. I don't know how productive I'll be or what that means to me. I'm more likely to sleep in until 11:00 a.m. and stay up until 2:00 a.m.

But if Anne Spencer has taught me anything, it's that I can just be. And simply being on my own terms is enough.

Notes

Introduction

1. Georgia Douglas Johnson to Anne Spencer, February 24, 1951, box 4, folder 6, Papers of Anne Spencer and the Spencer Family, 1829, 1864–2007, #14204, Special Collections, University of Virginia Library, Charlottesville.
2. Although Spencer never published a collection of her poetry, two collections exist: J. Lee Greene's biography *Time's Unfading Garden: Anne Spencer's Life and Poetry* (Baton Rouge: Louisiana State University Press, 1977); and Nina V. Salmon, ed., *Anne Spencer: "Ah How Poets Sing and Die!"* (Lynchburg, VA: Warwick House, 2001). I cite Greene's text because all subsequent scholarship on Anne Spencer rests on the shoulders of this foundational work.
3. See Deborah E. McDowell, *"The Changing Same": Black Women's Literature, Criticism, and Theory* (Bloomington: Indiana University Press, 1995); Maureen Honey, *Aphrodite's Daughters: Three Modernist Poets of the Harlem Renaissance* (New Brunswick, NJ: Rutgers University Press, 2016); and Gloria T. Hull, *Color, Sex, and Poetry: Three Women Writers of the Harlem Renaissance* (Bloomington: Indiana University Press, 1987).
4. Ecofeminism is defined as follows: "an umbrella term for a range of theoretical and practical positions that share the view that the 'twin dominations of women and nature' . . . are artifacts of patriarchal culture instituted in antiquity and . . . intensified by the epistemological dualism and rational instrumentalism of the scientific and technological revolutions" (Lawrence Buell, *The Future of Environmental Criticism: Environmental Crisis and Literary Imagination* [Hoboken, NJ: Blackwell, 2005], 139).
5. I use "colonial" to signal "colonization," the process of appropriating a geographical region for one's own use, which also involves domination over, removal of, and/or genocide of indigenous peoples. Within the context of this analysis, I am alluding to both the prehistory of the United States in British North America and colonization projects under nineteenth- and twentieth-century European and North American colonialism that rendered Black women an always-available natural resource to be exploited in various ways.
6. Because Spencer is a Black woman, it is reasonable to assume that her speakers are Black women as well, so I read her speakers as Black women in this work.

7. Throughout this volume, the terms "environmental imaginary" and "environmental consciousness" will be used interchangeably and very broadly to refer to the way in which one articulates their relationship to the natural world.

8. The project of reclamation is the focus of recent scholarship on Black engagement with the natural world, as is evident in the works of Kimberly N. Ruffin, *Black on Earth: African American Ecoliterary Traditions* (Athens: University of Georgia Press, 2010); Kimberly K. Smith, *African American Environmental Thought: Foundations* (Lawrence: University of Kansas Press, 2011); Carolyn Finney, *Black Faces, White Spaces: Reimagining the Relationship of African Americans to the Great Outdoors* (Chapel Hill: University of North Carolina Press, 2014); and Dianne D. Glave, *Rooted in the Earth: Reclaiming the African American Environmental Heritage* (Chicago: Chicago Review Press, 2010). Each of these scholars discusses the ways in which the natural world has been racialized as a white space in Western society's literary imagination. These authors contest the myth that African-descended individuals are anti-environmental and establish Blacks as possessing an environmental consciousness and being intimately and historically connected to the natural world. Though the aforementioned authors identify Black artists as environmentally conscious individuals, Black-authored texts are curiously underutilized and overlooked as possible primary sources within the bourgeoning field of literary ecocriticism.

9. Scholars such as Hazel Carby, Kimberly Wallace-Sanders, and Carla Peterson have examined how Black women have utilized literary forms to both redefine and challenge traditional notions of womanhood and create alternative definitions of Black womanhood that reflect their material conditions. A partial list includes Hazel Carby's *Reconstructing Womanhood: The Emergence of the Afro-American Woman Novelist* (New York: Oxford University Press, 1987); Kimberly Wallace-Sanders's edited volume *Skin, Deep, Spirit Strong: The Black Female Body in American Culture* (Ann Arbor: University of Michigan Press, 2002); Carla Peterson's *"Doers of the Word": African American Women Speakers and Writers of the North (1830–1880)* (New York: Oxford University Press, 199). Collectively, these texts examine how Black women have utilized discursive forms to both redefine and challenge traditional notions of womanhood and create alternative definitions of Black womanhood that reflect their material conditions. These authors identify a tradition within Black women's writing through which Black women writers both reclaim and recast representations of Black womanhood.

   Lawrence Buell defines ecocriticism as follows: "Ecocriticism is an umbrella term . . . used to refer to the environmentally oriented study of literature and (less often) the arts more generally, and to the theories that underlie such critical practice" (*The Future of Environmental Criticism,* 138). Buell explains that despite the "ancient roots" of environmental writing, ecocriticism is an emergent discourse, one that began in the late twentieth century (1–2). It is also sometimes abbreviated as "ecocrit." In this project, the terms "ecocriticism" and "ecoliterary criticism" will be used interchangeably.

10. "Ecopoetics" is something of a slippery term with no singular definition, and I cite Scott Knickerbocker's definition because it is both concise yet unrestrictive in its scope. Jonathan Skinner, editor of the journal *ecopoetics,* uses the following in his understanding of the term: "'Eco' here signals—no more, no less—the house we share with several million other species, our planet Earth. 'Poetics' is used as poesis or making, not necessarily to emphasize the critical over the creative act (nor vice versa). Thus: ecopoetics, a house making" (Skinner, *ecopoetics,* no. 1 [2001]: 7). Poet and literary critic Chris Arigo is careful to note, "Ecopoetics does not necessarily mean nature poetry" (Arigo, "Notes toward an Ecopoetics: Revising the Postmodern Sublime and Juliana Spahr's *This Connection of Everyone with Lungs." How2* 3, no. 2 [2008], http://www.asu.edu/pipercwcenter/how2journal/vol_3_no_2/index.html.4). Poet Juliana Spahr defines "ecopoetics" as follows: "a poetics full of systemic analysis and critique that questions the divisions between nature and culture while also acknowledging that humans use up too much of the world" (Spahr, *Things of Each Possible Relation Hashing against One Another* [Newfield, NY: Palm, 2003], 29). I offer these definitions to illustrate the myriad ways ecopoetics is deployed and to highlight that, at its core, ecopoetics seeks to theorize the relationship between individuals and the natural world. Therefore, my proposed expansion of the term is not only fitting but also essential if the full range of one's lived experience is to be considered.

11. Abel Meeropol is the author of "Strange Fruit"; sometimes the song is attributed to Lewis Allan, which is the pen name that he used to write songs and poetry (see Elizabeth Blair, "The Strange Story of the Man behind 'Strange Fruit,'" NPR.org, 5 September 2012, http://www.npr.org/2012/09/05/158933012/the-strange-story-of-the-man-behind-strange-fruit).

12. For a history of lynching in American literature and culture, see Jacqueline Goldsby, *A Spectacular Secret: Lynching in American Life and Literature* (Chicago: University of Chicago Press, 2006).

13. This term is adapted from Elizabeth Jane Harrison, *Female Pastoral: Women Writers Re-Visioning the American South* (Knoxville: University of Tennessee Press, 1991). In *Female Pastoral,* she uses this term to signal how women writers appropriated pastoral writing to articulate their unique female perspectives.

14. Spencer's birth name is "Annie Bethel Scales." Her birthname is also sometimes listed as "Annie Bethel Scales Bannister" (see Greene, chap. 1). James Weldon Johnson is credited for suggesting she use "Anne" for publication purposes, but she published her first story using "Anne" in 1900 before this suggestion was made. She did not meet Johnson until around 1918 (see Greene 49).

1. "'Leventy-Leven Bits Stuck in As Many Different Places"

1. Anne Spencer to James Weldon Johnson, October 20, 1921, on the back of a Johnson letter dated September 24, box 4, folder 7, Papers of Anne Spencer and the Spencer Family, 1829, 1864–2007, #14204, Special Collections, University of Virginia Library, Charlottesville.

2. Of Spencer's writing process, Greene notes, "Sometimes she would awake in the middle of the night and write something down somewhere—a 'habit' she never was able to break. Even some of the books in her library have their blank pages filled with lines of poetry, critical evaluations of or responses to ideas in the books, or 'just thoughts.' She remarked that she always had written primarily for her own enjoyment and not for publication or praise" (Greene, *Time's Unfading Garden: Anne Spencer's Life and Poetry* [Baton Rouge: Louisiana State University Press, 1977], 50). Greene also recalls an anecdote Spencer shared in which she spontaneously penned the poem "Dunbar" to teach her students about the fundamentals of poetry and suggests that Spencer's desire to expose children to literature may explain the some of the drafts of verses and stories seen in her archive (Greene 86).

3. University of Virginia acquired the Papers of Anne Spencer and the Spencer Family on March 10, 2008.

4. For Royster's precise periodization, see *Sounding Like a No-No: Queer Sounds & Eccentric Acts in the Post-Soul Era* (Ann Arbor: University of Michigan Press, 2013), 1–34.

5. I am aware that such an argument about eccentricity and alternate ways of "being" in the world gestures toward phenomenology (as well as other ontological theories), which is beyond the scope of this project. For a study of African American literature and phenomenology, see Charles Johnson, *Being and Race: Black Writing since 1970* (Bloomington: Indiana University Press, 1998).

6. For further discussion on the challenges of working within a Black woman's archive, see Saidiya Hartman, "Venus in Two Acts," *Small Axe* 12, no. 2 (2008): 1–14; Darlene Clarke Hine, "Rape and the Lives of Black Women in the Middle West: Preliminary Thoughts on the Culture of Dissemblance," in *Words of Fire: An Anthology of African American Feminist Thought*, ed. Beverly Guy-Sheftall (New York: New Press, 1995), 380–88; and Evelyn Brooks Higginbotham, "The Politics of Respectability," chapter 7 in *Righteous Discontent: The Women's Movement in the Black Baptist Church, 1880–1920* (Cambridge, MA: Harvard University Press, 1993).

7. Coined by civil rights and women's movement activist Pauli Murray, "Jane Crow" refers to how Black women experienced Jim Crow differently because of the intersection of the race and gender (see "Part III: Naming Jane Crow," in Rosalind Rosenberg, *Jane Crow: The Life of Pauli Murray* [New York: Oxford University Press, 2017]).

8. Shaun Spencer-Hester, Anne Spencer House and Garden Historic Museum tour, Lynchburg, Virginia, August 25, 2016.

9. Anne Spencer to Mr. Bosler, box 5, folder 13, Papers of Anne Spencer and the Spencer Family, 1829, 1864–2007, #14204, Special Collections, University of Virginia Library, Charlottesville.

10. The other two literary salons belonged to A'Leilia Walker and Georgia Douglas Johnson in New York and Washington, DC, respectively.

11. Greene notes that Spencer chose to limit her publications as opposed to succumb to editorial mandates. Though he, himself, describes Spencer's poetry as

not being "racially oriented" (128), he questions how freely pre-1940s Black artists were able to express themselves. Spencer admitted to him that she had written thousands of poems, which is in stark contrast to the approximately thirty published, anthologized poems. Greene notes that Spencer censored her poems to avoid controversy and that she was subjected to unwanted censorship of her protest poems. Most notably, her frequently anthologized poem "White Things" contained a reference to "white men," which the publishing editors deleted so that the poem would be published and not appear too controversial (see Greene, chap. 8).

12. In *Color, Sex, & Poetry in the Harlem Renaissance,* Gloria (Akasha) Hull writes extensively about the importance of the cultural labor of salon-keeping as an integral part of the artistic and cultural production of the period (see Hull, *Color, Sex, and Poetry: Three Women Writers of the Harlem Renaissance* [Bloomington: Indiana University Press, 1987], chap. 1).

13. Here I am drawing on Henry Louis Gates Jr.'s theorizing of signification theory within African American cultural expression in *Figures in Black:* "Signifying, it is clear, in black discourse means modes of figuration itself.... This rhetorical naming by indirection is, of course, central to our notions of figuration, troping, and of the parody of forms, or pastiche, in evidence when one writer repeats another's structure by one of several means, including a fairly exact repetition of a give narrative or rhetorical structure filled incongruously with a ludicrous or incongruent content" (Gates, *Figures in Black: Words, Signs, and the "Racial" Self* [New York: Oxford University Press, 1987], 236, 242).

14. W. E. B. Du Bois to Anne Spencer, December 19, 1927, W. E. B. Du Bois Papers (MS 312), Special Collections and University Archives, University of Massachusetts Amherst Libraries.

15. I encountered more manuscripts and revisions of this poem than any other poem, and based on her handwriting, it is a poem that she revised and revisited for several decades.

16. A letter from United States District Judge Alfred Dickinson Barksdale, dated December 18, 1956, excused her from jury duty on account of her arthritis (box 1, folder1); Robert Abernathy referenced her arthritis in a January 21, 1961, letter (box 1, folder 2). Mary M. Councell says, in a letter dated August 27, 1958, that she is sorry Spencer is having trouble with her hands (box 1, folder 4, Papers of Anne Spencer and the Spencer Family, 1829, 1864–2007, #14204, Special Collections, University of Virginia Library, Charlottesville).

17. For further reading on *embodied discourse,* see the prologue and pages 40–41 of *Beyond Respectability: The Intellectual Thought of Race Women* (Champaign: University of Illinois Press, 2017).

18. Anne Spencer to Mr. Bosler, undated, box 5, folder 13, Papers of Anne Spencer and the Spencer Family, 1829, 1864–2007, #14204, Special Collections, University of Virginia Library, Charlottesville.

19. For a historical and contemporary discussion of revolutionary mothering and radical mothering, see Alexis Pauline Gumbs, Gina Martens, and Mai'a

Williams, *Revolutionary Mothering: Love on the Front Lines* (Oakland, CA: PM, 2016).

20. For further information on Edward Spencer's work ethic, see Greene 44–45.

21. Anne Spencer, n.d., Poem "Amends," box 22, folder 1, Papers of Anne Spencer and the Spencer Family, 1829, 1864–2007, #14204, Special Collections, University of Virginia Library, Charlottesville. I have transcribed this poem to the best of my ability and included edits for clarity.

2. "This Small Garden Is Half My World"

1. The archive of Black feminist writers is too rich to provide an exhaustive list; however, see Ntozake Shange, *for colored girls who have considered suicide/when the rainbow is enuf* (New York: Scribner, 1974); Sonia Sanchez, *A Blues Book for Black Magical Women* (New York: Broadside, 1974); Toni Cade Bambara, *The Black Woman: An Anthology* (New York: New American Library 1970).

2. For a detailed discussion of the domestic sphere and white womanhood, see Barbara Welter's essay "The Cult of True Womanhood, 1820–1860," *American Quarterly* 18, no. 2 (1966): 151–74; and Linda M. Perkins, "The Impact of the 'Cult of True Womanhood' on the Education of Black Women," *Journal of Social Issues* 39, no. 3 (1983): 17–28.

3. For a detailed description of the garden in both its original form and its current state, see Rebecca T. Frischkorn and Reuben M. Rainey, *Half My World: The Garden of Anne Spencer* (Lynchburg, VA: Warwick House, 2003), chaps. 2 and 5.

4. Shaun Spencer-Hester, Anne Spencer House and Garden Historic Museum tour, Lynchburg, Virginia, August 25, 2016.

5. Anne Spencer, n.d., manuscript, box 20, folder 5, Papers of Anne Spencer and the Spencer Family, 1829, 1864–2007, #14204, Special Collections, University of Virginia Library, Charlottesville.

3. "God Never Planted a Garden"

1. Anne Spencer, n.d., manuscript, box 20, folder 5, Papers of Anne Spencer and the Spencer Family, 1829, 1864–2007, #14204, Special Collections, University of Virginia Library, Charlottesville.

2. Anne Spencer, n.d., manuscript. box, 20, folder 5, Papers of Anne Spencer and the Spencer Family, 1829, 1864–2007, #14204, Special Collections, University of Virginia Library, Charlottesville.

3. See Delores S. Williams, "Sin, Nature, and Black Women's Bodies," in *Ecofeminism and the Sacred,* ed. Carol J. Abrams (London: Continuum, 1993), 24–29; and Shamara Shantu Riley, "Ecology Is a Sistah's Issue, Too," ibid., 191–204.

4. In other parts of this work, I have referred to Spencer's politics as "feminist" and "Black feminist" where appropriate. For a discussion on the differences between these terms, see Patricia Hill Collins "What's in a Name? Womanism,

Black Feminism, and Beyond," *Black Scholar* 26, no. 1 (1996): 9–17; bell hooks, *Talking Back: Thinking Feminist, Thinking Black* (Boston: South End, 1989), 181–82; Alice Walker, *In Search of Our Mothers' Gardens* (New York: Harcourt, 1983), xi; Jacqueline Grant "Womanist Theology: Black Women's Experience as a Source for Doing Theology, with Special Reference to Christology," in *African American Religious Studies: An Interdisciplinary Anthology,* ed. Gayraud Wilmore (Durham, NC: Duke University Press, 1989), 208–27; Stacey Floyd-Thomas, introduction to *Deeper Shades of Purple: Womanism in Religion and Society,* ed. Floyd-Thomas (New York: New York University Press, 2006), 1–14.

5. For more information about Spencer's civil rights activism in Lynchburg, Virginia, see J. Lee Greene, *Time's Unfading Garden: Anne Spencer's Life and Poetry* (Baton Rouge: Louisiana State University Press, 1977), chap. 6.

6. I also draw upon Ruffin's definition of "ecology": *"the study of the often overlapping experience of relationships among humans and among humans and non-human nature.* Ecology as it is used in this book, presupposes that (1) humans are indeed 'natural'; (2) humans have developed a powerful and distinct culture with nature; and (3) cultural definitions of 'humanity' influence an individual's experiences among humans and with non-human nature" (18; emphasis original).

7. See Katie Cannon, *Black Womanist Ethics* (Atlanta: Scholars Press, 1988); Delores S. Williams, *Sisters in the Wilderness: The Challenge of Womanist God-Talk* (Maryknoll, NY: Orbis Books, 1993); Judylyn S. Ryan, *Spirituality as Ideology in Black Women's Film and Literature* (Charlottesville: University of Virginia Press, 2005); Yvonne P. Chireau, *Black Magic: Religion and the African American Conjuring Tradition* (Berkeley: University of California Press, 2003); bell hooks, *Sisters of the Yam: Black Women and Self-Recovery* (Cambridge: South End, 2005), chaps. 12 and 13.

8. Carter asserts five "core principles" of Black women's spiritual autobiographies. The above core principle is the third, and the remaining are as follows: "First, the genre of spiritual autobiography offers paradigmatic framework for the divine heroine to obtain spiritual faculty through personal transformation. . . . Secondly, spiritual autobiographies and modern spiritual works articulate experience that encourage activism on behalf of the godhead. . . . Fourthly, the consistent, restorative, and bold renderings of contemporary authors mark their immense popularity. . . . Finally, black women authors provide the most demonstrative but not the sole tradition of black feminist divinity" (Tomeiko Ashford Carter, *Powers Divine: Spiritual Autobiography and Black Women's Writing* [Lanham, MD: University Press of America, 2009], xv–xix).

9. *Merriam-Webster.com Dictionary,* s.v. "commune," https://www.merriam-webster.com/dictionary/commune.

10. Georgia Douglas Johnson to Anne Spencer, February 24, 1951, box 4, folder 6, Papers of Anne Spencer and the Spencer Family, 1829, 1864–2007, #14204, Special Collections, University of Virginia Library, Charlottesville.

11. Anne Spencer, n.d., handwritten manuscript, "Love and Gardens," quoted on p. 1, box 17, folder 32, Papers of Anne Spencer and the Spencer Family, 1829, 1864–2007, #14204, Special Collections, University of Virginia Library, Charlottesville. The page numbers cited refer to Spencer's handwritten pagination on the manuscript.

12. For further reading on representations of Black female bodies in literature and culture, see Michael Bennet and Vanessa D. Dickerson, eds., *Recovering the Black Female Body: Self-Representations by African American Women* (New Brunswick, NJ: Rutgers University Press, 2001).

13. For further reading on the spirituality, namely African spiritual practices, in Toni Morrison's novels, see K. Zauditu-Selassie's *African Spiritual Traditions in the Novels of Toni Morrison* (Gainesville: University of Florida Press, 2009).

14. Anne Spencer, "The Adviser" (December 1970), box 12, folder 1, Papers of Anne Spencer and the Spencer Family, 1829, 1864–2007, #14204, Special Collections, University of Virginia Library, Charlottesville. I transcribed this poem to the best of my ability and included edits for clarity.

15. *Merriam-Webster.com Dictionary*, s.v. "impinge," https://www.merriam -webster.com/dictionary/impinge.

16. Examples of biblical conversion stories include (but are not limited to) "The Woman at the Well" in John 4: 4–26; the story of Zacchaeus the Tax Collector in Luke 19:1–10; and the Conversion of Paul the Apostle in Acts 9:1–19.

17. Scripture quotations marked (NIV) are taken from the Holy Bible, New International Version®, NIV®. Copyright © 1973, 1978, 1984, 2011 by Biblica, Inc.™ Used by permission of Zondervan. All rights reserved worldwide. www. zondervan.com. The "NIV" and "New International Version" are trademarks registered in the United States Patent and Trademark Office by Biblica, Inc.™

18. Anne Spencer, n.d., manuscript, box 5, folder 13, Papers of Anne Spencer and the Spencer Family, 1829, 1864–2007, #14204, Special Collections, University of Virginia Library, Charlottesville.

19. Anne Spencer, n.d., manuscript, box 20, folder 5, Papers of Anne Spencer and the Spencer Family, 1829, 1864–2007, #14204, Special Collections, University of Virginia Library, Charlottesville.

20. See Genesis 1:31 and Exodus 20:13.

21. An alternative, gender-inclusive translation is: "is humanity's number." For further reading on the "Mark of the Beast," see Revelation 13; Revelation 16:2; and Revelation 19:20. In many Christian traditions, this enigmatic "Mark of the Beast" has been associated with the antichrist and those who worship the antichrist.

22. *Merriam-Webster.com Dictionary*, s.v. "plant," https://www.merriam-webster .com/dictionary/plant.

23. Anne Spencer, n.d., manuscript, box 20, folder 5, Papers of Anne Spencer and the Spencer Family, 1829, 1864–2007, #14204, Special Collections, University of Virginia Library, Charlottesville.

24. The Gnostic Gospels consist of fifty-two texts discovered in 1945 near the Egyptian town of Naj Hammadi. In her seminal work *The Gnostic Gospels* (New

York: Random House, 1979), scholar Elaine Pagels writes, "These diverse texts range, then, from secret gospels, poems, and quasi-philosophic descriptions of the origin of the universe, to myths, magic and instructions for mystical practice" (xvii). Such texts as *The Gospel of Thomas* are titled, but the author of *Thunder, Perfect Mind* is unknown but is believed to be the female voice of God. For further reading on the Gnostic Gospels and gnostic faith, see Pagels, *The Gnostic Gospels.*

4. "I Proudly Love Being a Negro Woman"

1. In this chapter, I use the terms "New Negro Movement" and "New Negro Renaissance" interchangeably to refer to the literary and cultural movement that occurred from approximately World War I to the late 1930s.
2. See W. E. B. Du Bois, "The Study of the Negro Problems," *Annals of the American Academy of Political and Social Science* (1898): 1–23; and W. E. B. Du Bois, *The Souls of Black Folk. The Three Negro Classics* (New York: Avon, 1965), 207–389.
3. See Maureen Honey, *Shadowed Dreams: Women's Poetry of the Harlem Renaissance* (New Brunswick, NJ: Rutgers University Press, 1989); Gloria T. Hull, *Color, Sex, and Poetry: Three Women Writers of the Harlem Renaissance* (Bloomington: Indiana University Press, 1987); Deborah E McDowell, *"The Changing Same": Black Women's Literature, Criticism, and Theory* (Bloomington: Indiana University Press, 1995); Cheryl A. Wall, *Women of the Harlem Renaissance* (Bloomington: Indiana University Press, 1995).
4. For the entire story, see J. Lee Greene, *Time's Unfading Garden: Anne Spencer's Life and Poetry* (Baton Rouge: Louisiana State University Press, 1977), 41–42.
5. Other notable literary influences include Ralph Waldo Emerson, Olive Schreiner, Henry David Thoreau, James Weldon Johnson, Emily Dickinson, Paul Laurence Dunbar, and John Brown. For a full list and discussion of Spencer's literary influences see Greene 1, 36, 48–66, 90, 108–12, 123, 94–95, 141–43, 168–73.
6. Greek mythology seems to have been an area of interest and source of inspiration for New Negro Renaissance women writers (although it is beyond the realm of my project to argue this definitively). In *Aphrodite's Daughters,* Maureen Honey writes that poets Gwendolyn Bennet, Mae Cowdery, and Angelina Grimké appropriated Aphrodite and imagined her as a Black woman in their erotic poetry (see Honey, *Aphrodite's Daughters: Three Modernist Poets of the Harlem Renaissance* [New Brunswick, NJ: Rutgers University Press, 2016], 6–12).
7. Greene notes: "Actually, Edward's middle name was not Alexander. He was named Edward Boyd Spencer, but when he entered the seminary he changed it to E.A.—Edward Alexander, after Alexander the Great" (43).
8. For an in-depth analysis and history of masking, see Rafia Zafar, *We Wear the Mask: African Americans Write American Literature, 1760–1870* (New York: Columbia University Press, 1997).
9. These are the names of English Romantic poets: Thomas Chatterton, Percy Bysshe Shelley, and John Keats. As her biographer explains, Spencer composed

this poem while she was "conducting an exercise with some small children whom she was trying to teach rudimentary techniques of literature and especially of poetry. . . . Some time after this, she sent the poem enclosed with a letter to Johnson who, after reading it, responded: 'As soon as I opened it and found the little poem on [Paul Laurence] Dunbar, I immediately took the lines over to the *Crisis* office. They wanted very much to print the poem under Dunbar's picture in the June number, but found it was too late as the forms had been locked up.' . . . This incident not only reveals Anne Spencer's interest in introducing children to literature, but it also suggests that the scarcity of literature for children motived her to write, as is evidenced by several drafts of verses and stories which could have been written for such a purpose" (Greene 86; see also chap. 6).

10. Anne Spencer, n.d., manuscript, "Modern Poetry," box 17, folder 34, Papers of Anne Spencer and the Spencer Family, 1829, 1864–2007, #14204, Special Collections, University of Virginia Library, Charlottesville.

5. Do Not Separate Them from Their Gardens

1. In my use of "poetics," I am referring to theory and practice of studying linguistic techniques in literature. This should be distinguished from "discourse," which I am using to signal the existence of a body of scholarship on the subject of Black women's writers' self-representation.

2. For a discussion of Hurston's impact on Walker, see the essays "Zora Neale Hurston: A Cautionary Tale and a Partisan View" and "Looking for Zora" in Alice Walker, *In Search of Our Mothers' Gardens* (New York: Harcourt, 1983).

3. It bears noting that such scholars as John S. Mbiti have noted the prevalence of tree imagery and tree tropes in West African Spiritual cultures as well (see Mbiti's seminal work *African Religions & Philosophy* [New York: Doubleday Anchor, 1970]).

4. For further reading on Janie's self-creation, see McKinley Melton, "What God Hath Put Together: Hurston, Black Queer Love, and the Act of Creation," *Langston Hughes Review* 26, no. 1 (2020): 1–28.

5. See Zora Neale Hurston, "What White Publishers Won't Print," in *African American Literary Theory: A Reader,* ed. Winston Napier (New York: New York University Press, 2000), 54–57.

6. This term is adapted from Scott Hicks's essay. He uses the term "ecovisionary" to describe Hurston's spiritual, creative use of natural world symbols (see Scott Hicks, "Zora Neale Hurston: Environmentalist in Southern Literature," *"The Inside Light": New Critical Essays on Zora Neale Hurston,* ed. Deborah G. Plant [New York: Praeger, 2010], 113–25).

Coda

1. Anne Spencer, n.d., manuscript, box 20, folder 5, Papers of Anne Spencer and the Spencer Family, 1829, 1864–2007, #14204, Special Collections, University of Virginia Library, Charlottesville.

2. Georgia Douglas Johnson to Anne Spencer, 24 February 1951, box 4, folder 6, Papers of Anne Spencer and the Spencer Family, 1829, 1864–2007, #14204, Special Collections, University of Virginia Library, Charlottesville.

3. Anne Spencer, n.d., manuscript, box 20, folder 5, Papers of Anne Spencer and the Spencer Family, 1829, 1864–2007, #14204, Special Collections, University of Virginia Library, Charlottesville.

Bibliography

Abbandonato, Linda. "'A View from 'Elsewhere': Subversive Sexuality and the Rewriting of the Heroine's Story in *The Color Purple*." *PMLA* 106, no. 6 (1991): 1106–15. JSTOR, http://www.jstor.org/stable/462683.

"Anne Spencer House and Garden Museum." www.annespencermuseum.com/.

Arigo, Christopher. "Notes toward an Ecopoetics: Revising the Postmodern Sublime and Juliana Spahr's *This Connection of Everyone with Lungs*." *How2* 3, no. 2 (2008). http://www.asu.edu/pipercwcenter/how2journal/vol_3_no_2 /index.html.

Armbruster, Karla, and Kathleen R. Wallace. "Introduction: Why Go Beyond Nature Writing, and Where To?" In *Beyond Nature Writing: Expanding the Boundaries of Ecocriticism,* edited by Armbruster and Wallace, 1–28. Charlottesville: University of Virginia Press, 2001.

Baker, Houston A., Jr. *Modernism and the Harlem Renaissance.* Chicago: University of Chicago Press, 1987.

Bambara, Toni Cade. *The Black Woman: An Anthology.* New York: New American Library, 1970.

Baver, Sherrie L., and Barbara Deutsch Lynch. "The Political Ecology of Paradise." In *Beyond Sun and Sand: Caribbean Environmentalisms,* edited by Baver and Lynch, 3–17. New Brunswick, NJ: Rutgers University Press, 2006.

Bennett, Michael, and Vanessa D. Dickerson, eds. *Recovering the Black Female Body: Self-Representations by African American Women.* New Brunswick, NJ: Rutgers University Press, 2001.

Biondi, Martha. *To Stand and Fight: The Struggle for Civil Rights in Postwar New York City.* Cambridge, MA: Harvard University Press, 2003.

Blair, Elizabeth. "The Strange Story of the Man behind 'Strange Fruit.'" September 5, 2012. http://www.npr.org/2012/09/05/158933012/the-strange-story-of-the-man -behind-strange-fruit.

Boyce-Davies, Carole, and Molara Ogundipe-Leslie. Introduction to *Moving beyond Boundaries,* vol. 1: *International Dimensions of Black Women's Writing,* edited by Boyce-Davies and Ogundipe-Leslie, 1–17. New York: New York University Press, 1995.

Bracks, Lean'tin L., and Jessie Carney Smith, eds. *Black Women of the Harlem Renaissance Era.* Lanham, MD: Rowman and Littlefield, 2014.

Brand, Dionne. *In Another Place, Not Here.* New York: Grove, 1996.

Buell, Lawrence. *The Environmental Imagination: Thoreau, Nature Writing, and the Formation of American Culture*. Cambridge, MA: Harvard University Press, 1995.

———. *The Future of Environmental Criticism: Environmental Crisis and Literary Imagination*. Hoboken, NJ: Blackwell, 2005.

Cannon, Katie. *Black Womanist Ethics*. Atlanta: Scholars Press, 1988.

Carby, Hazel V. *Reconstructing Womanhood: The Emergence of the Afro-American Woman Novelist*. New York: Oxford University Press, 1987.

Carter, Tomeiko Ashford. *Powers Divine: Spiritual Autobiography and Black Women's Writing*. Lanham, MD: University Press of America, 2009.

Chapman, Erin D. *Prove It on Me: New Negroes, Sex, and Popular Culture in the 1920s*. New York: Oxford University Press, 2012.

Cheng, Annie. *Second Skin: Josephine Baker and the Modern Surface*. New York: Oxford University Press, 2011.

Chireau, Yvonne Patricia. *Black Magic: Religion and the African American Conjuring Tradition*. Berkeley: University of California Press, 2003.

Christian, Barbara. "The Race for Theory." *Feminist Studies* 14, no. 1 (1988): 67–79. JSTOR, http://www.jstor.org/stable/3177999.

Cohen, Cathy J. "Punks, Bulldaggers, and Welfare Queens: The Radical Potential of Queer Politics?" *GLQ: A Journal of Lesbian and Gay Studies* 3, no. 4 (1997): 437–65.

Collier-Thomas, Bettye. *Jesus, Jobs, and Justice: African American Women and Religion*. New York: Knopf, 2010.

Cooper, Brittney C. *Beyond Respectability: The Intellectual Thought of Race Women*. Champaign: University of Illinois Press, 2017.

Cullen, Countee, ed. *Caroling Dusk: An Anthology of Verse by Negro Poets*. New York: Citadel, 1993.

Cvetkovich, Ann. *An Archive of Feelings: Trauma, Sexuality, and Lesbian Public Cultures*. Durham, NC: Duke University Press, 2003.

Du Bois, W. E. B. *The Souls of Black Folk*. *The Three Negro Classics*. New York: Avon, 1965.

———. "The Study of the Negro Problems." *Annals of the American Academy of Political and Social Science* (1898): 1–23.

Dunbar, Paul Laurence. "Sympathy." In *The Collected Poetry of Paul Laurence Dunbar*, edited by Joanne M. Braxton, 314. Charlottesville: University of Virginia Press, 1993.

———. "We Wear the Mask." In *The Collected Poetry of Paul Laurence Dunbar*, edited by Joanne M. Braxton, 71, Charlottesville: University of Virginia Press, 1993.

Dunbar-Nelson, Alice. "I Sit and Sew." In *Caroling Dusk: An Anthology of Verse by Black Poets of the Twenties*, edited by Countee Cullen. 73. New York: Citadel, 1993.

Dunning, Stefanie K. *Black to Nature: Pastoral Return and African American Culture*. Jackson: University of Mississippi Press, 2021.

Egar, Emmanuel E. *Black Women Poets of the Harlem Renaissance*. Lanham, MD: University Press of America, 2003.

Fauset, Jessie Redmon. *Plum Bun: A Novel without a Moral.* Boston: Beacon, 1999.

Finney, Carolyn. *Black Faces, White Spaces: Reimagining the Relationship of African Americans to the Great Outdoors.* Chapel Hill: University of North Carolina Press, 2014.

Floyd-Thomas, Stacey M. Introduction to *Deeper Shades of Purple: Womanism in Religion and Society,* edited by Floyd-Thomas, 1–14. New York: New York University Press, 2006.

Ford, Charita. "Flowering a Feminist Garden: The Writings and Poetry of Anne Spencer." *SAGE* 5, no. 1 (1988): 7–14.

Frischkorn, Rebecca T., and Reuben M. Rainey. *Half My World: The Garden of Anne Spencer.* Lynchburg, VA: Warwick House, 2003.

Gates, Henry Louis, Jr. *Figures in Black: Words, Signs, and the "Racial" Self.* New York: Oxford University Press, 1987.

———. *The Signifying Monkey: A Theory of African American Literary Criticism.* New York: Oxford University Press, 1988

Genovese, Eugene. *Roll, Jordan, Roll: The World the Slaves Made.* New York: Vintage, 1976.

Glave, Dianne D. "Black Environmental Liberation Theology." In *"To Love the Wind and Rain": African Americans and Environmental History,* edited by Glave and Mark Stoll, 189–99. Pittsburgh, PA: University of Pittsburgh Press, 2006.

———. "Eco-Theology in the African Diaspora." In *The Wiley Blackwell Companion to Religion and Ecology,* edited by John Hart, 85–89. New York: John Wiley and Sons, 2017.

———. *Rooted in the Earth: Reclaiming the African American Environmental Heritage.* Chicago: Chicago Review Press, 2010.

Goldsby, Jacqueline. *A Spectacular Secret: Lynching in American Life and Literature.* Chicago: University of Chicago Press, 2006.

Gomez, Michael. *Exchanging Our Country Marks.* Chapel Hill: University of North Carolina Press, 1998.

Grant, Jacquelyn. "Womanist Theology: Black Women's Experience as a Source for Doing Theology, with Special Reference to Christology." *African American Religious Studies: An Interdisciplinary Anthology,* edited by Gayraud Wilmore, 208–27. Durham, NC: Duke University Press, 1989.

Greene, J. Lee. *Time's Unfading Garden: Anne Spencer's Life and Poetry.* Baton Rouge: Louisiana State University Press, 1977.

Grewal, Gurleen. "Beholding 'A Great Tree in Leaf': Eros, Nature, and the Visionary in *Their Eyes Were Watching God.*" In *"The Inside Light": New Critical Essays on Zora Neale Hurston,* edited by Deborah G. Plant, 103–12. New York: Praeger, 2010.

Gumbs, Alexis Pauline, China Martens, and Mai'a Williams, eds. *Revolutionary Mothering: Love on the Front Lines.* Oakland, CA: PM, 2016.

Harris, William J. *The Leroi Jones/Amiri Baraka Reader.* New York: Thunder's Mouth, 1991.

Harris-Perry, Melissa V. *Sister Citizen: Shame, Stereotypes, and Black Women in America.* New Haven, CT: Yale University Press, 2011.

Harrison, Elizabeth Jane. *Female Pastoral: Women Writers Re-Visioning the American South*. Knoxville: University of Tennessee Press, 1991.

Hartman, Saidiya. "Venus in Two Acts." *Small Axe* 12, no. 2 (2008): 1–14.

Hicks, Scott. "Zora Neale Hurston: Environmentalist in Southern Literature." In *"The Inside Light": New Critical Essays on Zora Neale Hurston,* edited by Deborah G. Plant, 113–25. New York: Praeger, 2010.

Higginbotham, Evelyn Brooks. *Righteous Discontent: The Women's Movement in the Black Baptist Church, 1880–1920*. Cambridge, MA: Harvard University Press, 1993.

Hill Collins, Patricia. "What's in a Name? Womanism, Black Feminism, and Beyond." *Black Scholar* 26, no. 1 (1996): 9–17.

Hine, Darlene Clark. "Rape and the Inner Lives of Black Women in the Middle West: Preliminary Thoughts on the Culture of Dissemblance." In *Words of Fire: An Anthology of African American Feminist Thought,* edited by Beverly Guy-Sheftall, 380–88. New York: New Press, 1995.

Hobson, Janell. "The 'Batty' Politic: Toward an Aesthetics of the Black Female Body." *Hypatia* 18, no. 4 (2003): 87–105.

Honey, Maureen. *Aphrodite's Daughters: Three Modernist Poets of the Harlem Renaissance*. New Brunswick, NJ: Rutgers University Press, 2016.

———. Introduction to *Shadowed Dreams: Women's Poetry of the Harlem Renaissance,* edited by Honey, 1–41. New Brunswick, NJ: Rutgers University Press, 1989.

hooks, bell. *Sisters of the Yam: Black Women and Self-Recovery*. Cambridge: South End, 2005.

———. *Talking Back: Thinking Feminist, Thinking Black*. Boston: South End, 1989.

Huebener, Paul, and Dionne Brand. "'No Moon to Speak Of': Identity and Place in Dionne Brand's *In Another Place, Not Here.*" *Callaloo* 30, no. 2 (2007): 615–25. JSTOR, http://www.jstor.org/stable/30129775.

Hughes, Langston. "My Adventures as a Social Poet." *Phylon* 8, no. 3 (1947): 205–12.

Hull, Gloria T. *Color, Sex, and Poetry: Three Women Writers of the Harlem Renaissance*. Bloomington: Indiana University Press, 1987.

Hurston, Zora Neale. "How It Feels to Be Colored Me." In *The Norton Anthology of African American Literature,* 3rd. ed., edited by Henry Louis Gates Jr. and Valerie A. Smith, 1:1040–42. New York: Norton, 2014.

———. *Their Eyes Were Watching God*. New York: Harper and Row, 1937.

———. "What White Publishers Won't Print." In *African American Literary Theory: A Reader,* edited by Winston Napier, 54–57. New York: New York University Press, 2000.

Hyest, Jenny. "Anne Spencer's Feminist Modernist Poetics." *Journal of Modern Literature* 38, no. 3 (2015): 120–47.

Johnson, Charles. *Being and Race: Black Writing since 1970*. Bloomington: Indiana University Press, 1988.

Johnson, Georgia Douglas. "The Heart of a Woman." In *Caroling Dusk: An Anthology of Verse by Black Poets of the Twenties,* edited by Countee Cullen, 81. New York: Citadel, 1993.

Johnson, Helene. "Sonnet to a Negro in Harlem." In *Caroling Dusk: An Anthology of Verse by Black Poets of the Twenties,* edited by Countee Cullen, 217. New York: Citadel, 1993.

Johnson, James Weldon, ed. *The Book of American Negro Poetry.* New York: Brace and World, 1931.

Jones, Martha S. *All Bound up Together: The Woman Question in African American Public Culture, 1830–1900.* Chapel Hill: University of North Carolina Press, 2007.

Karapetkova, Holly. "'Chatterton, Shelley, Keats and I': Reading Anne Spencer in the White Literary Tradition." *Callaloo* 35, no. 1 (2012): 228–44. Project MUSE, DOI: 10.1353/cal.2012.0018.

Knickerbocker, Scott. *Ecopoetics: The Language of Nature, the Nature of Language.* Amherst: University of Massachusetts Press, 2012.

Lewis, Christopher S. "Cultivating Black Lesbian Shamelessness: Alice Walker's *The Color Purple*." *Rocky Mountain Review* 66, no. 2 (2012):158–75. JSTOR, http://www.jstor.org/stable/41763555.

Litwack, Leon. *Been in the Storm So Long: The Aftermath of Slavery.* New York: Vintage, 1979.

Lorde, Audre. *A Burst of Light and Other Essays.* Ann Arbor, MI: Firebrand, 1988.

———. *Sister Outsider.* Berkeley, CA: Crossing, 1984.

Marouan, Maha. *Witches, Goddesses, and Angry Spirits: The Politics of Spiritual Liberation in African Diaspora Women's Fiction.* Columbus: Ohio State University Press, 2020.

Mbiti, John S. *African Religions and Philosophy.* New York: Doubleday Anchor, 1970.

McDougald, Elise Johnson. "The Task of Negro Womanhood." In *The New Negro,* edited by Alain Locke, 370–82. New York: Simon and Schuster, 1925.

McDowell, Deborah E. "Afterword: Recovery Missions: Imaging the Body Ideals." In *Recovering the Black Female Body: Self-Representations by African American Women,* edited by Michael Bennet and Vanessa D. Dickerson, 296–318. New Brunswick, NJ: Rutgers University Press, 2001.

———. *"The Changing Same": Black Women's Literature, Criticism, and Theory.* Bloomington: Indiana University Press, 1995.

———. Introduction to *Plum Bun: A Novel without a Moral,* ix–xxxiii. Boston: Beacon, 1999.

McKay, Claude. "If We Must Die." In *Double-Take: A Revisionist Harlem Renaissance Anthology,* edited by Venetria K. Patton and Maureen Honey. New Brunswick, NJ: Rutgers University Press, 2001.

McKittrick, Katherine. *Demonic Grounds: Black Women and the Cartographies of Struggle.* Minneapolis: University of Minnesota Press, 2006.

McKittrick, Katherine, and Clyde Woods, eds. *Black Geographies and the Politics of Place.* Boston: South End, 2007.

Melton, McKinley. "What God Hath Put Together: Hurston, Black Queer Love, and the Act of Creation." *Langston Hughes Review* 26, no. 1 (2020): 1–28.

Morgan, Jennifer L. *Laboring Women: Reproduction and Gender in New World Slavery.* Philadelphia: University of Pennsylvania Press, 2004.

Outka, Paul. *Race and Nature from Transcendentalism to the Harlem Renaissance.* New York: Palgrave Macmillan, 2008.

Pagels, Elaine. *The Gnostic Gospels.* New York: Random House, 1979.

Patterson, Tiffany Ruby, and Robin D. G. Kelley. "Unfinished Migrations: Reflections on the African Diaspora and the Making of the Modern World." *African Studies Review* 43, no. 1 (2000): 11–45.

Perkins, Linda M. "The Impact of the 'Cult of True Womanhood' on the Education of Black Women." *Journal of Social Issues* 39, no. 3 (1983): 17–28.

Peterson, Carla L. *"Doers of the Word": African American Women Speakers and Writers of the North (1830–1880).* New York: Oxford University Press, 1995.

———. "Foreword: Eccentric Bodies." In *Recovering the Black Female Body: Self-Representations by African American Women,* edited by Michael Bennett and Vanessa D. Dickerson, ix–xvi. New Brunswick, NJ: Rutgers University Press, 2001.

Quashie, Kevin Everod. *The Sovereignty of Quiet: Beyond Resistance in Black Culture.* New Brunswick, NJ: Rutgers University Press, 2012.

Quynn, Kristina. "Elsewheres of Diaspora: Dionne Brand's *In Another Place, Not Here.*" *Journal of the Midwest Modern Language Association* 48, no. 1 (2015): 121–46.

Riley, Shamara Shantu. "Ecology Is a Sistah's Issue, Too." In *Ecofeminism and the Sacred,* edited by Carol J. Abrams, 191–204. London: Continuum, 1993.

Rosenberg, Rosalind. *Jane Crow: The Life of Pauli Murray.* New York: Oxford University Press, 2017.

Roses, Lorraine Elena, and Ruth Elizabeth Randolph, eds. *Harlem's Glory: Black Women Writing 1900–1950.* Cambridge, MA: Harvard University Press, 1997.

Royster, Francesca T. *Sounding Like a No-No: Queer Sounds & Eccentric Acts in the Post-Soul Era.* Ann Arbor: University of Michigan Press, 2013.

Ruffin, Kimberly N. *Black on Earth: African American Ecoliterary Traditions.* Athens: University of Georgia Press, 2010.

Ryan, Judylyn S. *Spirituality as Ideology in Black Women's Film and Literature.* Charlottesville: University of Virginia Press, 2005.

Sanchez, Sonia. *A Blues Book for Black Magical Women.* New York: Broadside, 1974.

Scales, Anne Bethel. "Beth's Triumph (*A Two-Part Story*)." Part 1. *Colored American Magazine* 1, no. 3 (August 1900): 152–59. HathiTrust Digital Library.

———. "Beth's Triumph (*A Two-Part Story*)." Part 2. *Colored American Magazine* 1, no. 4 (September 1900): 238–44. HathiTrust Digital Library.

Schwarz, A. B. Christa. *Gay Voices of the Harlem Renaissance.* Bloomington: Indiana University Press, 2003.

Shange, Ntozake. *A Daughter's Geography.* New York: St. Martin's, 1983.

———. *For colored girls who have considered suicide/when the rainbow is enuf.* New York: Scribner, 1975.

Sherrard-Johnson, Cherene. *Portraits of the New Negro Woman: Visual and Literary Culture in the Harlem Renaissance.* New Brunswick, NJ: Rutgers University Press, 2007.

Shockley, Evie. *Renegade Poetics: Black Aesthetics and Formal Innovation in African American Poetry.* Ames: University of Iowa Press, 2011.

Skinner, Jonathan, ed. *ecopoetics,* no. 1. New York: Periplum, 2001.

Smethurst, James. *The African American Roots of Modernism: From Reconstruction to the Harlem Renaissance.* Chapel Hill: University of North Carolina Press, 2011.

Smith, Kimberly K. *African American Environmental Thought: Foundations.* Lawrence: University of Kansas Press, 2007.

Spahr, Juliana. *Things of Each Possible Relation Hashing against One Another.* Newfield, NY: Palm, 2003.

Spencer, Anne. "Love and Gardens." Undated, handwritten manuscript. Papers of Anne Spencer and the Spencer Family, 1829, 1864–2007. #14204. Special Collections, University of Virginia Library, Charlottesville.

Spencer, Anne, and the Spencer Family, 1829, 1864–2007. Papers. #14204. Special Collections, University of Virginia Library, Charlottesville.

Spillers, Hortense. "Mama's Baby, Papa's Maybe: An American Grammar Book." *Diacritics* 17, no. 2 (1987): 64–81.

Stallings, L. H. *Funk the Erotic: Transaesthetics of Black Sexual Cultures.* Champaign: University of Illinois Press, 2015.

Stetson, Erlene. "Anne Spencer." *College Language Association Journal* 21 (1978): 400–409.

Taylor, Ula. "Women in the Documents: Thoughts on Uncovering the Personal, Political, and Professional." *Journal of Women's History* 20, no. 1 (2008): 187–96. Project MUSE, DOI: 10.1353/jowh.2008.0010.

Walker, Alice. *The Color Purple.* Orlando, FL: Harcourt, 1982.

———. *In Search of Our Mothers' Gardens.* New York: Harcourt, 1983.

Wall, Cheryl A. *Women of the Harlem Renaissance.* Bloomington: Indiana University Press, 1995.

Wallace-Sanders, Kimberly, ed. *Skin Deep, Spirit Strong: The Black Female Body in American Culture.* Ann Arbor: University of Michigan Press, 2002.

Welter Barbara, "The Cult of True Womanhood: 1820–1860." *American Quarterly* 18, no. 2 (1966): 151–74.

West, Elizabeth J. *African Spirituality in Black Women's Fiction: Threaded Visions of Memory, Community, Nature and Being.* Lanham, MD: Lexington, 2011.

Williams, Delores S. "Sin, Nature, and Black Women's Bodies." In *Ecofeminism and the Sacred,* edited by Carol J. Abrams, 24–29. London: Continuum, 1993.

———. *Sisters in the Wilderness: The Challenge of Womanist God-Talk.* Maryknoll, NY: Orbis Books, 1993.

Wintz, Cary D. "Harlem Renaissance: 1920–1940." In *Women Artists of the Harlem Renaissance,* edited by Amy Helene Kirschke, 3–21. Jackson: University Press of Mississippi, 2014.

Zafar, Rafia. *We Wear the Mask: African Americans Write American Literature, 1760–1870.* New York: Columbia University Press, 1997.

Zauditu-Selassie, K. *African Spiritual Traditions in the Novels of Toni Morrison.* Gainesville: University of Florida Press, 2009.

Index

Du Bois, W. E. B., 12, 13, 23, 25, 52, 80.
    See also New Negro Renaissance;
    Souls of Black Folk, The (Du Bois)
"Dunbar" (Spencer), 18, 78, 98–99,
    132n2, 137n9
Dunbar, Paul Lawrence, 21, 92, 98,
    137n5, 137n9
Dunbar High School, 33
Dunbar-Nelson, Alice, 81, 91–92, 97, 98
Dunning, Stefanie K., 122

"[Earth, I thank you]" (Spencer), 13, 38,
    43–45, 53
ecocriticism. *See* literary ecocriticism
ecotheology, 60, 67, 75, 76
Edankraal, 22, 46, 52, 55
Ellison, Ralph, 87
Emerson, Ralph Waldo, 7, 137n5
Environmental Imagination, The
    (Buell), 7

Faulkner, William, 87
Fauset, Jessie Redmon, 3–4, 42, 53, 54,
    55, 81. *See also* New Negro woman
Female Pastoral (Harrison), 8–9
feminism: and Black environmental
    liberation theology (BELT), 76; and
    Black feminism, 2, 3, 4, 5–6, 15, 19,
    38, 39, 40, 42–43, 56, 60, 66, 68, 76,
    80, 81, 85, 85–86, 88, 122, 134–35n4,
    134n1; and Black feminist epistemol-
    ogy, 19, 38, 121; and ecofeminism, 5,
    14, 44, 104, 129n4; and modernism,
    94–95; and mulatta figure, 88; and
    Anne Spencer, 4, 5, 14, 19, 40, 42–43,
    60, 66, 80, 81, 90, 94–95, 100, 121. *See
    also* womanism
Finney, Carolyn, 7–8, 40
Fitzgerald, F. Scott, 87
Ford, Charita M., 4
"For E.A.S." (Spencer), 98–99
Frischkorn, Rebecca T., 34, 39, 48, 50,
    52, 134n3
Frost, Robert, 87

gardening: and African American
    vernacular gardens, 50–51; and
    African American women, 49, 53,
    55; and crossbreeding of plants, 52;
    and cultivation of writing, 27, 34,
    52–53; and *Dreer's Garden Book*, 52;
    and God, 36, 65, 68; and ideologies
    of dominion, 50; and importance of
    to Spencer, 3, 18, 49, 65–66, 126; *joy*
    of, 49; and mothering, 32, 33; and the
    natural world, 50; and transplanting
    from the wild, 50
Gates, Henry Louis, Jr., 133n13
gender: and "Before the Feast at
    Shushan" (Spencer), 94; and Black
    women, 9, 10, 70, 84–85, 119; and
    Black women's literature, 2, 9, 10, 11,
    54, 55, 91, 97, 119; and ecocriticism,
    15, 119; and gender equality, 54, 55,
    97; and gender politics, 13–14, 38,
    95, 99; and gender relations, 4, 55;
    and God's gender, 67, 77, 136n23; and
    Jane Crow, 132n7; and Janie Craw-
    ford (character), 106; and marriage
    roles, 98; and mulatta figure, 88, 90;
    and nature, 5, 9, 10, 106; and oppres-
    sion, 2; in pastoral writing, 8–9; and
    queer studies, 15; and Anne Spencer,
    31; and Spencer's poetry, 99, 100, 101,
    102; and "the Negro problem," 83
Glave, Diane D., 42, 59, 60
Gnostic Gospels, The (Pagels), 77
"[God never planted a garden]" (Spen-
    cer), 73–77
Gomez, Michael, 60
Greene, J. Lee: and Anne Spencer's
    leisure time, 32; and Anne Spencer's
    routine, 33; and Edward Spencer, 32,
    137n7; and Spencer's biography, 3, 36,
    60, 63, 90, 95, 129n2; and Spencer's
    poetry, 42, 129n2; and Spencer's writ-
    ing, 132–33n11; and Spencer's writing
    process, 17–19, 21, 23, 132n2. See also
    Time's Unfading Garden (Greene)

Grewal, Gurleen, 106, 108
Grimké, Angelina Weld, 101, 137n6

Harper, Frances E. W., 105
Harrison, Elizabeth Jane, 8–9
Harris-Perry, Melissa, 114
Hemingway, Ernest, 87
"He Said" (Spencer), 13, 38, 54, 55
Hine, Darlene Clarke, 20
Hobson, Janell, 108
Holiday, Billie, 9
Honey, Maureen, 3, 5, 84, 86, 91, 99
hooks, bell, 62
Hopkins, Pauline, 105
Hughes, Langston, 13, 51, 80
Hull, Gloria (Akasha), 3, 5, 86, 133n12
Hurston, Zora Neale: and Black
    womanhood, 104, 110, 118–19;
    environmental consciousness of,
    104–5; influence on Alice Walker,
    138n2; natural world writing of, 14,
    99, 103–4, 118–19, 138n6; "pastoral-
    ism," 7; and "What White Publishers
    Won't Print," 112, 138n5
Hyest, Jenny, 4, 79, 94. See also "Anne
    Spencer's Feminist Modernist Poet-
    ics" (Hyest)

In Another Place, Not Here (Brand), 14,
    103, 104, 114–18
In Search of Our Mothers' Gardens
    (Walker), 24, 36, 63–64, 138n2

Jena Six case, 11
Johnson, Georgia Douglas: and Black
    women's literature, 81, 91, 92, 95, 96,
    97–98; and letter to Anne Spencer,
    1, 8, 15, 64, 124; literary salon of,
    132n10; and New Negro Movement,
    13, 80, 86; and Spencer's garden, 51
Johnson, Helene, 81
Johnson, James Weldon: death of, 25; as
    friend and editor, 25, 26, 79, 88, 125,
    131n14; and Spencer's letters, 17, 21,

22, 23, 26, 27, 30, 131n1, 137n9; and
    Spencer's writing, 12, 22, 23, 25, 26,
    30, 102, 137n5, 137n9

Karapetkova, Holly, 4, 46–47, 94, 96,
    97
Keats, John, 4, 78, 84, 98, 137n9

Laboring Women (Morgan), 41
Larsen, Nella, 3–4, 42, 53, 54, 55, 81. See
    also New Negro woman
"Lines to a Nasturtium (A Lover
    Muses)" (Spencer), 100–102
literary ecocriticism: and Afro-
    diasporic women's writing, 8, 14; and
    Black-authored texts, 130n8; and
    Black female writers, 1, 8–10, 11, 14,
    99, 130n9; and Black womanhood,
    11, 14, 130n9; and colonialism, 11; and
    difference, 11, 14; and ecocriticism,
    130n9; and ecopoetics, 2, 8–10, 11, 13,
    14, 15, 131n10; and lived experience,
    10, 11, 131n10; and the natural world,
    10–11, 14–15, 131n10; and Spencer's
    writing, 121, 122; and trauma, 10, 11
Litwack, Leon, 61
Lorde, Audre, 32, 34, 40, 63, 68, 69. See
    also sexuality
"Love and Gardens" (Spencer): con-
    version in, 72; and creativity, 68;
    and ideologies of dominion, 68; and
    motherhood, 39, 65; and the natural
    world, 36, 65, 66, 74; and Papers
    of Anne Spencer and the Spencer
    Family, 136n11; and parenting, 65, 66,
    68; and Spencer's conception of God,
    66–68, 70, 73, 76
Lynchburg, Virginia: and Anne Spencer
    House and Garden Museum, 124, 125,
    132n8, 134n4; and Jim/Jane Crow,
    63; and Anne Spencer, 60, 63, 64, 86,
    135n5; Edward Spencer in, 32; and
    Spencer's garden, 51, 63, 122, 125; Spen-
    cer's home in, 3, 13, 22, 32, 41, 86, 125

Quashie, Kevin, 9, 82
queer studies, 15, 19, 101, 122

race: and African American experience, 100, 123, 134n1; and Ahmaud
Arbery, 123; and "Before the Feast
at Shushan" (Spencer), 94; and
Black eccentricity, 20, 56; and Black
womanhood, 5–6, 10, 41, 42, 56–57,
83–84; and Black women's literature,
2, 10, 20, 41, 56–57; and colonialism,
10; and critical race studies, 9; and
ecocriticism, 15, 119; and the environment, 11, 40–41, 123; and environmental racism, 11, 59; and God, 71;
and Jim/Jane Crow, 20, 22, 34, 126,
127, 132n7; and lynching, 131n12; and
mulatta figure, 87, 88, 89, 90; and the
natural world, 7–8, 10–11, 41, 44, 99,
122–24, 130n8; and New Negro wom-
en's discourse, 53, 83–85; and northern
United States, 122; and oppression, 2,
10, 84, 85, 88, 91; in pastoral writing,
8–9; and race-mothers, 84; and
racialized nature, 10; and racism, 11,
59, 84, 94, 122, 127; and the Romantic
sublime, 10; and Spencer's poetry,
100, 101, 133n11; and Spencer's writing, 31, 56–57, 58, 73, 80, 81, 82–83, 95;
and "the Negro problem," 4, 82–83;
and white supremacy, 73, 75–76; and
white womanhood, 134n2. See also
"White Things" (Spencer)
*Race and Nature from Transcenden-
talism to the Harlem Renaissance*
(Outka), 9–10
Rainey, Reuben M., 34, 39, 48, 50, 52,
134n3
religion: and African religions, 60–61,
138n3; and the Bible, 40, 72, 75,
76, 136n16, 136n20; and the Black
church, 61; and Black environmental
liberation theology (BELT), 59–60,
76; and Black liberation theology,
59–60; and Black women's writing,

61–64, 66–72, 77–78, 135n8, 136n13;
and Christianity, 59, 60–61, 64, 68,
72, 74, 76, 77, 136n20; and the divine
Black woman, 66, 67, 68–69, 75, 76,
77, 135n8; and ecotheology, 60, 67,
75, 76; and enslaved people, 61; and
gnostic tradition, 77, 136n23; and
God, 13, 40, 58–59, 60, 61, 64–72, 73,
74–76, 77, 78, 103, 107, 124, 136n23;
and ideologies of dominion, 40,
59, 66, 72–73; and importance of
solitude, 62–63; and Jesus Christ, 61;
and liberation theology, 59–60, 61;
and the natural world, 13, 40, 59–60,
61; and theology, 13, 18, 58, 59–61, 67.
See also ecotheology
Renegade Poetics (Shockley), 5, 82
Riley, Shamara Shantu, 59
Ruffin, Kimberly N., 60, 119, 130n8,
135n6

Sanchez, Sonia, 32, 40
sexuality: and Black sexuality, 55–56, 84,
108, 111–12; and Black womanhood, 2,
3–4, 10, 83, 84, 85, 88, 92, 104–5, 108,
112–18, 119; and Black women's literature, 2, 10, 84, 85, 91, 92, 101, 104–5,
108, 109–12; and Celie (character),
111, 112, 113–14, 118; and ecocriticism,
15; and Elizete (character), 115, 117–18;
and homosexuality, 101; and Janie
Crawford (character), 105–10, 118; and
lesbian/gay archives, 20, 30–31; and
liberation, 54, 85; and Lorde's notion
of the erotic, 115; and mulatta figure,
88; and the natural world, 5, 9, 11; and
New Negro womanhood, 3–4, 54,
85, 92; and non-normative sexuality,
11, 12, 101–2, 112, 118–19; in pastoral
writing, 8; and queerness, 101, 117–18,
119; and sexual autonomy, 5, 10, 85, 88,
99; and theory of *funky erotixxx*, 9.
See also queer studies
Shadowed Dreams (Honey), 99
Shange, Ntozake, 40, 68–69

Shelley, Percy Bysshe, 4, 78, 98, 137n9

slavery: and Adela (character), 116; Black people in, 44; and Black women, 5, 41, 49–50, 62, 64, 111, 126; and colonization, 42; conditions under, 117; and "cult of domesticity and true womanhood," 49–50; and ideologies of dominion, 42; and liberation theology, 61; and the Middle Passage, 61; and physical abuse, 9; and Spencer's writing, 18; tropes of, 87

"Sonnet to a Negro in Harlem" (Johnson), 92–94

Souls of Black Folk, The (Du Bois), 96

Sounding Like a No-No (Royster), 19–20

Spencer, Anne: and anthropocentrism, 59, 72–73; archive of, 8, 12, 13, 15, 17, 18, 19, 20, 21–23, 24, 25, 26, 27, 28–35, 36, 43, 52, 58, 59, 60, 62, 67, 69, 72, 78, 80, 118, 122, 123, 124, 127, 132n2; arthritis of, 30, 126, 133n16; and beauty, 48, 66; and *being*, 38, 62, 68, 78, 122, 126, 127, 132n5; belief in equality of, 5, 123; and Black feminism, 2, 4, 6, 14, 122; and Black womanhood, 1, 2–3, 4, 5, 6, 7, 11, 12, 13–14, 19, 20–21, 32, 34, 36, 38, 39–40, 42, 46, 56–57, 64–65, 66, 67, 68, 75, 76–78, 80, 81, 89–91, 94, 95–99, 121; and Black women's literary studies, 121–22, 129n6; and Browning's poetry, 46, 47; children of, 32, 33, 34, 35, 36, 127; and civil rights, 3, 14, 35, 59, 81, 125, 135n5; correspondence of, 12–13, 17, 21, 22, 23, 25–27, 30, 80, 82, 133n14, 133n16, 133n18, 135n10, 137n9, 138n2; daily life of, 19, 33, 37, 52–53, 62, 122, 126; death of, 25, 69, 72, 122; eccentricity of, 12, 17, 18, 19–20, 21, 22, 24, 28, 30, 31, 32, 37, 62, 63, 122, 124, 132n5; and ecopoetics, 2, 13, 38, 40, 58; and embodied discourse, 31, 67, 133n17; environmental consciousness of, 2, 8, 12, 13, 14, 28, 42–43, 45, 56–59, 81, 99, 100, 123, 130n7; and

fragmentary writing, 24, 25–26, 29, 126; garden of, 1, 2, 3, 4, 6, 8, 12, 13, 15, 18, 22, 23, 27, 30, 33, 34, 36, 37, 38–39, 41, 42, 46, 47, 48, 49, 50–52, 53, 54, 55, 58, 59, 60, 62, 63, 65–66, 81, 99, 100, 103, 122, 123, 124, 134n3; and happiness, 3, 14, 39, 42, 53, 121; and Harlem, New York, 86; identity of, 14, 23, 36, 81, 125; and ideologies of dominion, 41, 43, 100–101, 123; and immortality, 48; and Jim/Jane Crow era, 32, 126, 127; language of, 26, 28, 37, 38, 43, 44, 46, 48, 53, 71, 81, 96, 98, 100, 101; and legibility, 6, 18–19, 20, 21, 22, 28, 29, 30, 81–82, 98, 102, 126, 127; as a librarian, 14, 33, 81, 125; and literary ecocriticism, 121, 122; literary salon of, 12–13, 22, 36, 80, 86, 123, 125; and love, 13, 48, 55, 65, 68, 76, 78, 97, 98, 100; and "manyness," 21, 26–27; and marriage to Edward, 32, 34, 35, 55, 90, 98; and matrimony, 13, 32, 55, 97–98; mixed-race ancestry of, 58, 73; and modernism, 4–5, 12, 13–14, 24, 46–47, 79–88, 91, 94, 97, 99, 100, 102; and motherhood, 31–34, 35, 36, 63, 65, 125; mulatta iconography of, 89–90; name of, 15, 88, 131n14; and the natural world, 1, 2, 3, 4, 5, 6–8, 11–12, 13, 14, 18, 19, 36, 38–39, 40, 41, 42, 43–52, 55, 56, 57, 58–59, 60, 62, 63, 64, 65–66, 68, 72, 74–75, 76, 77, 81, 99, 99–100, 101, 104, 121, 122, 123–24; and New Negro womanhood, 54, 55; numbers in verse of, 73–74; and Papers of Anne Spencer and the Spencer Family, 4, 12, 17, 18, 27–28, 29, 50, 52, 123, 124, 126, 131n1, 132n3, 132n9, 133n16, 133n18, 138n3; and parenting, 13, 14, 18, 31, 32, 35, 36, 65, 66; and poem "The Wife-Woman," 73; poetry of, 1, 2, 3, 4–5, 6, 7, 8, 12, 13, 14, 15, 17, 18, 22–23, 25, 27, 28, 31, 32, 34–49, 50, 52, 53, 54–55, 56, 57, 58, 59, 62, 65, 69–80, 81, 82, 94–102,

118, 121–22, 124, 125, 126, 127, 129n2, 132–33n11, 132n2, 133n14; politics of, 2, 4, 13–14, 18, 29, 60, 99, 134–35n4; and privacy, 6, 21–22, 24–26, 27, 28, 35; prose writing of, 1–2, 3, 4, 12, 18, 25, 27, 28, 30, 39, 59, 62, 67, 81, 82, 121, 122, 125, 126, 127; and publication, 4, 12, 15, 18, 23–27, 28, 30, 39, 57, 58, 64, 121–22, 126, 127, 129n2, 132–33n11, 132n2; and self-care, 33, 34, 40, 53, 56, 63, 121, 126; and self-creation, 106, 126; short stories of, 88; and space-making, 2, 6–7, 8, 12, 17, 18–19, 22, 46, 78, 80, 82, 122; spirituality of, 13, 36, 58–59, 60, 62, 63, 64–65, 66, 67, 68, 72–73, 77–78, 124; and teaching, 18, 33, 66, 132n2, 137–138n9; and theology, 58–59, 60, 62, 63, 64, 66, 67–69, 75, 76, 78; and use of wild plants, 52; writing process of, 17–19, 20, 22, 23, 24, 25–26, 132n2. *See also* ecotheology; feminism
Spencer, Chauncey (son), 33, 34, 127
Spencer, Edward: businesses of, 32–33, 126; environmental consciousness of, 55; and gardening, 52, 55; home of, 32, 125; and marriage to Anne, 35, 55; name of, 137n7; and Spencer's poetry, 54, 55–56, 97; work ethic of, 134n20
Spencer, Sarah (mother), 90
Stallings, L. H., 9
Stein, Gertrude, 87
Stetson, Erlene, 4

Taylor, Ula, 13, 20
Teasdale, Sara, 84
Their Eyes Were Watching God (Hurston): and Black women, 10, 14, 77, 103, 109–11, 118; and ecofeminism, 104; and ecopoetics, 106, 111, 118; Janie Crawford (character), 103, 105–11, 112, 113, 114, 117, 118, 138n4; and

the natural world, 106–9, 110, 111, 112, 118; and New Negro Movement, 86; and self-creation, 110–11, 138n4; and Shug Avery (character), 107
Thoreau, Henry David, 7, 137n5
Thurman, Howard, 80
Time's Unfading Garden (Greene), 3, 129n2, 137n4
Toomer, Jean, 7, 87
Truth, Sojourner, 85

"Unfinished Migrations: Reflections on the African Diaspora and the Making of the Modern World" (Kelley), 14

Virginia Theological Seminary and College, 33

Walker, Alice: and Black womanhood, 45, 104, 111, 118–19; and creativity, 36, 64, 122; environmental consciousness of, 104–5; and lived experience, 24; natural world writing of, 14, 103–4, 111, 118–19; and womanism, 63, 111. See also *Color Purple, The* (Walker); Hurston, Zora Neale; *In Search of Our Mothers' Gardens* (Walker)
Wall, Cheryl A., 3, 5, 84, 86, 91
Wallace, Kathleen R., 10–11, 105
West, Elizabeth J., 61, 62
Wheatley, Phillis, 51, 61
"White Things" (Spencer), 76, 133n11
Williams, Delores S., 59, 75, 134n3
Witches, Goddesses, and Angry Spirits (Morrison), 68
Without Sanctuary (photojournalism), 9
womanism, 59, 60, 63, 111, 134–35n4
World War I, 12, 85, 100
World War II, 127

Yeats, William Butler, 47

CPSIA information can be obtained
at www.ICGtesting.com
Printed in the USA
BVHW041703110423
662158BV00014B/306